BIELSA = LEEDS

by

Michael Gill

CHAPTER 1

As It Was in the Beginning

On a lovely summer evening in June 2018, I was sat with two good friends in John Benny's Bar in Dingle County Kerry. We were enjoying a well earned pint after walking about ten miles on Inch Strand. Now don't get me wrong about these guys, they're both great fellows. I've known Mike and Graham for more than half a lifetime but they are not, how could I put it; enlightened. By this I mean that one supports Queens Park Rangers and the other Liverpool.

To my right was an empty bar stool and draped over the back was a Leeds United Training Top of a certain vintage. Its owner appeared shortly afterwards and after exchanging the Leeds salute, we proceeded to discuss the momentous happenings at Elland Road.

The two previous seasons had brought hope, at least at the beginning. In 2016-2017 Gary Monk had taken the team on an exciting journey only to fall away at the final stages.

In 2017 – 2018, the likeable Thomas Chritiansen's side had started like a house on fire but had imploded after the turn of the year as the side was plagued by injuries and indiscipline.

He was followed by the unfortunate Paul Heckingbottom who only succeeded in making matters worse. Two weeks earlier, Heckingbottom had been sacked as manager. He had had one of the shortest rides on the Leeds managerial merry go round but unlike some of his recent predecessors, in the Cellino era, he was likely to be compensated for his efforts without having to go to Court.

The newcomer, a loquacious Dubliner informed me that Leeds had finally announced the appointment of Marcelo Bielsa as First Team Coach and to my shame, he knew far more about Bielsa than I did.
My excuse was that I needed to be sure that the appointment was really going to happen before I did any serious research.

Somehow Victor Orta (Director of Football) and Andrea Radrizzani (Owner) had the neck to approach the Man from Rosario to talk to him about their vacancy: A move almost as bold as the late Bill Fotherby's aborted attempt to sign Maradonna. Whilst Fotherby had about as much chance of signing the American singer with the cone shaped bra, Orta and Radrizzani had actually succeeded in their quest.

Bielsa had famously managed a succession of Argentine Clubs between 1990 and 1998 before managing the national side between 1998 and 2004. He then managed the Chilean national side between 2007 and 2011 before coming to Europe to manage Atletico Bilbao and later Marseille.
It is fair to say that he enjoyed cult status and was worshipped by fans at all of these appointments, although his tenure at Marseille was cut short after a policy disagreement with the management. Whilst his trophy count is not high, his coaching methods have been widely praised and copied throughout the world.

In July 2016 he joined Lazio, only to walk away after two days, claiming that the club had reneged both on signing the players that he wanted as well as allowing a large number of existing players to leave the club. His next appointment at Lille (2017) lasted a little over seven months. His contract was terminated after a run of poor results. The club's owners felt that Bielsa's insistence on clearing out some of the older players and relying on youth was to blame for this. It was clear then, that this maverick of a man would need careful handling by the Leeds ownership.

It was widely assumed that the protracted negotiations that took place between Leeds and Bielsa at the time were due to haggling over the size of payment package needed to bring their man over from the other side of the World.

Nothing could have been further from the truth: Bielsa was showing his new employers the amount of research that he had already done on the EFL Championship in general and in Leeds United in particular. This was a portent of things to come. His sheer thoroughness and attention to detail would be a feature of his tenure from day one.

About a week later, Bielsa held his first press conference. He was introduced by Andrea Radrizzani, who made clear that the Argentine's influence would spread from top to bottom at the club and would also cover the Academy.

Bielsa intimated that he had already watched all fifty one of United's games the previous season and that he was of the opinion that he club needed strengthening in four or five areas. He also said that as many as fifteen players would have to be disposed of because he did not want players that he was not using in the squad. When asked about promotion to the Premier League, he pointed out politely that it would be imprudent of him to make such a forecast at this stage but that it was certainly a dream. He came across as a modest and humble man, who was able to show these character traits only because he had complete confidence in himself.

As the keyboard warriors of social media went into overdrive, complaining about the lack of incoming signings, a quiet revolution was taking place. Intensive training sessions followed, the players were divided into three groups: The First Team Squad, The Development Squad, and a third group which consisted of the players that Bielsa had identified as being surplus to requirements. The unwanted group were given an extra week off in order to assist them to find new clubs.

Dark mutterings were heard about 9am to 7pm training sessions and players were accommodated in a local hotel to cut down on their travelling time. Rooms would later be arranged on site at Thorpe Arch Training Centre to facilitate this still further.

The cream of the academy players including Ryan Edmonson, Jamie Shackleton and Jack Clarke were already training with the top group and integration was on its way. The 'People's Republic of Thorpe Arch' was no more and it was clear that Bielsa believed that if players were good enough, then they were old enough.

A key move in this direction was the appointment of Carlos Corberan as First Team Coach, with Special Responsibilities for The Development Squad. Carlos has since proved to be the ideal conduit between the two groups, providing Bielsa with a seamless connection. Corberan had joined Leeds in 2017 as Under Twenty Three Coach under Thomas Christiansen.

The first opportunity that fans had to see the characters in the new regime was at a friendly match on 17th July against Forest Green Rovers at their picturesque ground above Nailsworth in Gloucestershire. The game had been previously been arranged as part of a deal which brought promising youngster Jordan Stevens to Leeds. Stevens had played nine games for Forest Green after bursting into the first team from their development squad.

I could think of a lot of good reasons for attending this match: Firstly, all football fans are getting very twitchy by this time of the year, having been deprived of their weekly 'fix' for at least ten weeks! Secondly I was fascinated by what I had heard of Bielsa and wanted to experience his coaching methods first hand and thirdly, I had never been to the ground before and it was an opportunity to add to my tally of football league grounds.

Therefore on a sunny July afternoon I took a leisurely drive through the beautiful Cotswolds to Nailsworth. I had booked a room at the Kings Head in Stonehouse which was a few miles away but was cheap and had good reviews. The plan was to check in, go to the match and then enjoy a couple of pints chatting to the locals in the cosy bar. Upon arriving, I noticed that the inn had all these things but the barman informed me that the bar would close at nine o'clock in the evening!

Undeterred, I made my way back to Nailsworth and parked my car in the town centre. After a bracing walk up a very steep hill, I arrived at Forest Green's ground. It was good to see a number of familiar faces all filled with the same feelings of anticipation, hope and optimism which is experienced by football fans at the start of (nearly) every season. The Leeds contingent supplied approximately 33% of the attendance.

The Leeds United team was as follows:
Peacock – Farrell, Ayling, Cooper, Beradi, Forshaw, Phillips, Dallas, Alioski, Saiz, Hernandez, Roofe.
Substitutes: Miazek, Dalby, Diaz & Rey.

Kemar Roofe opened the scoring on 16 minutes followed by a 'collector's piece' goal from Luke Ayling on 25 minutes. The unfortunately named Grubb equalised for Forest Green on the stroke of half time.

United dominated throughout the game but could not score any more goals. The most significant thing about this game was that Bielsa brought a tight squad to this game and did not use any of the substitutes. It was therefore a fair assumption that the players selected would form the core of his team for the new season unless there were spectacular and significant moves in the Summer Transfer Window.

This fact in itself led to muttering amongst the less positive of our colleagues but a win is a win.
After the game, I enjoyed a few pints with an old friend, Steve Heasman. Steve was staying in the Egypt Mill Hotel in Nailsworth. I left my car and got a taxi to Stonehouse and Steve graciously picked me up next morning and took me back to my car.

The next game was on 19th July against York City at Bootham Crescent. Bielsa fielded a completely different team; this team was a mixture of youngsters and those with something to prove along with Chelsea loanee Lewis Baker.

Leeds Team: Miazek (Huffer 45), De Bock, Ideguchi, Viera, Baker, Klich, Pearce, Clarke, Edmonson (Dalby 45), Shackleton, Stevens (Diaz 45). Unused Substitute: Rey.

An unnamed trialist scored for York on 23 minutes and Dalby equalised for Leeds on 57 minutes after Klich had hit the cross-bar. The main things gleaned from this game were a standout performance from Matteus Klich closely followed by Tom Pearce, Jack Clarke and Jamie Shackleton. Another talking point was the inclusion of Ronaldo Viera in this group rather than in the first team selections.

On July 22nd United travelled to Southend and again Bielsa brought a tight squad with him.

Leeds United: Peacock – Farrell, Ayling, Cooper, De Bock (Roberts 62), Beradi, Forshaw, Phillips, Alioski, Saiz, Dallas, Roofe. Unused Subs: Miazek, Edmondson & Stevens.

This was another unexceptional performance with few clues about what was to occur in the coming season. Lennon scored for Southend on twenty minutes, Luke Ayling equalising fourteen minutes later and had another cleared off the line near the end. Both Saiz and Roofe had come close earlier but the Whites had to be happy with a draw. Tyler Roberts came on after 62 minute as Leeds tried to chase the game. Tyler was given a warm welcome from the travelling fans as his Leeds career had never really got started after serious injury.

Two days later, the 'B' squad travelled to Oxford.

Leeds United: Huffer, (Blackman 45), Shackleton, Diaz, Rey, Pearce, Klich, Viera, Ideguchi (Roberts 45), Baker, Clarke, Dalby (Edmonson 45). Unused Substitute: Stevens.

Oxford powered into a 3 - 0 lead before half time with goals from Henry and Hall (2). After the break, Huffer made way for Chelsea loanee Jamal Blackman who was widely expected to replace Peacock - Farrell as first choice goalkeeper. Tyler Roberts replaced Ideguchi and Ryan Edmonson replaced Dalby.
Roberts (54) and Baker (63) reduced the deficit to one goal before

Oxford took the lead again through Obika. Leeds came back with all guns blazing and Jack Clarke scored ten minutes later. Unfortunately it was too little too late and the Whites had to go home empty – handed.

The final workout for Bielsa's 'A' Squad was on July 29th at home to Spanish side Las Palmas.

Leeds United: Peacock – Farrell, Ayling, Beradi, Cooper, Dallas, Phillips, Viera (Baker 45) (Shackleton 88), Alioski (Roberts 64), Saiz, (Klich 45) Hernandez, Roofe.
Unused Subs: Blackman, Huffer, Pearce & Clarke.

The first half was unexceptional in terms of chances for either side but I can honestly say that I was beginning to understand what the new coach's tactics were all about: United had completely dominated the midfield in particular and possession in general. In the 86th minute, Hernandez took a corner and Kalvin Phillips flicked a header on to Kemar Roofe who sorted his feet out and tapped the ball home from close range. This action allowed the 11,500 crowd to make their way home in good spirits although at this stage it has to be said that many were far from convinced that they were watching a side that would be challenging for promotion.

United had signed the following players:

Lewis Baker: Chelsea (loan)
Jamal Blackman: Chelsea (loan)
Jack Harrison: Manchester City (loan)
Patrick Bamford: Middlesbrough (undisclosed fee)
Barry Douglas: Wolves (undisclosed fee)
Izzy Brown Chelsea: (loan)

The following players were transferred out:

Madger Gomes: Sochaux (undisclosed fee)
Felix Wiedwald: Eintracht Frankfurt (undisclosed fee)
Marcus Antonsson: Malmo (undisclosed fee)

Andy Lonergan (released)
Mallik Wilks: Doncaster (loan)
Paudie O'Connor: Blackpool (loan)
Tyler Denton: Peterborough (loan)
Jay – Roy Grot: VVV Venlo (loan)
Pawel Cibicki: Molde (loan)
Lewie Coyle: Fleetwood (loan)
Luke Murphy: Bolton (free)
Ronaldo Viera: Sampadoria (undisclosed fee)
Hadi Sacko: Las Palmas (loan)
Yosuke Ideguchi: SPVgg Greuther Furth (loan)
Laurens de Bock: KV Oostende (loan)
Caleb Ekuban: Trabzonspor (loan)
Vurnon Anita: Willem 11 (loan)
Eunan O'Kane: Luton Town (loan)

This clearout showed a confidence and clarity of purpose not seen from a Head Coach at Leeds for a number of years. Few of the fans shed any tears for the departing players with one major exception. Ronaldo Viera was a favourite and had showed considerable promise. At his best he had a vision and range of passing which belied his tender years. Nevertheless, the Directors saw fit to accept a fee in the region of £7 million from Sampadoria.

Was this to be the first rift between Bielsa and the Board? Not a bit of it: He stated that although he rated Viera, he felt that the group could get on all right without him.

The other concern that was held by a lot of observers was that the squad was a small one when judged on previous standards. The area of concern was in the centre of defence. Bielsa did not go along with this thinking and even appeared to suggest to Victor Orta that he did not need to pursue anyone else unless an exceptional talent became available. We were to learn about his extraordinary ability to coach players to successfully perform in a variety of positions.

CHAPTER 2

August 2018 – Down to Business

The match day experience at Elland Road is still an authentic one. The current owners have done a good job in making the exterior of the Stadium far more attractive. The huge graphics which cover the stands were installed the previous season. Bremner Square now has hundreds of inscribed slate grey stones. Fans flocked to have their names and those of their loved ones included. The base of the Billy Bremner statue was always a focal point but now even more so. Fan Zones and extra bars have been set up to cope with the increasing demand for refreshments. Nevertheless, the old ground retains a vibrancy lost by many of the carbon copy new build stadia.

A 'hell fire and damnation' lay preacher still plies his trade, offering free tickets to a celestial Premier League to those who chose to seek the true path! There is also a piper in full tartan adding to the atmosphere.

My own personal match day experience is fairly repetitive and predictable. It starts as I join the 'Chiltern Whites' supporters coach in Luton. This supporter's branch has been ably run by Hector MacFarlane for a number of years. The coach driver, Elliott is also a dyed in the wool Leeds supporter.
My fellow travellers are a mixture of Yorkshire expats like myself and people from the South East who started supporting the Whites back in the Glory Years.

On reaching Leeds I walk up to the White Hart at Beeston, a pub that I have known since childhood as I went to school a few hundred yards away.

At weekends, I would often wait outside the White Hart for my father. I would have a bag of crisps, a snotty nose and a bottle of lemonade. Today it will be a couple of pints and some good conversation about the coming game. The current Landlord, Quentin keeps an excellent pint of Tetley's. He ensures the consistent quality by pulling all the Cask Ale pints himself as his staff handle the money and dispense the other beers.

After leaving the White Hart, I walk down Wesley Street from Beeston Hill which still retains its magic. The thrill when the East Stand comes into view, the hum of conversation from my fellow fans as they make their way towards the Sacred Shrine. The smell of the fried onions from the hotdog stands and the 'beep' as the turnstile accepts my season ticket. To go inside, mount the steps and greet people like Andy, Matt and Wendy, Steve, Ethan and Macker that I see every couple of weeks. Then we sing 'Marching on Together' in unison with the masses. There are no cardboard clappers or false bonhomie here. This is the real thing and completely spontaneous.

Leeds United 3 v Stoke City 1

August 5th 2018

Leeds United
Peacock – Farrell, Ayling, Beradi, Cooper, Phillips, Douglas, Klich (Dallas 76), Hernandez, Alioski (Harrison 89), Saiz (Baker 88) Roofe.
Unused Substitutes: Blackman, Janssen, Roberts Bamford.

Stoke City

Butland, Baur, Shawcross, Martins Indi, Pieters, Ndiaye (Fletcher 63) Etebo (Bojan 63), Allen, Ince, Afobe (Crouch 76), McClean.
Unused Substitutes: Williams, Diouf, Edwards, Federici.

Referee: S Duncan.

Attendance: 34,126

The main talking points before the match were the selection of Peacock – Farrell as goalkeeper. Jamal Blackman, on loan from Chelsea was widely expected to replace the young keeper but clearly had not passed Bielsa's conditioning process. Also on the bench were Pontus Jansson and Patrick Bamford. Jansson had been granted a couple of weeks extra holiday after representing Sweden in the World Cup.

Bamford, who was United's most expensive signing in many years also kept the bench warm. It was clear that players had to go through the coach's full induction process before appearing in the starting team. Therefore the starters, with the exception of Douglas and Klich were pretty well the same side that had under-achieved the previous season.

Stoke, having been relegated from the Premier League had started the season as one of the hot favourites to return there at the first attempt. They had a strong squad and Manager Gary Rowett was highly rated.

What happened next was almost cruel. KLICH (15) opened the scoring after receiving a defence splitting pass from Saiz. For the remainder of the first half, United battered the Stoke defence and were rewarded on the stroke of half time when HERNANDEZ (45 + 1) slipped the ball through the clutching fingers of Butland. Previously, a shot from Tom Ince had grazed the bar, albeit totally against the run of play.

Shortly after half time, AFOBE (52) put away a penalty after Ince had been brought down but this seemed to encourage United to get back on the front foot. This they did, COOPER (57) heading home from a Barry Douglas corner. The Bielsa era had started with a convincing win.

Both at the post Stoke and pre Derby press conferences journalists slowly learned not to ask Bielsa clichéd questions. This proved to be a difficult task for many of them. Not that he cut them down with sarcastic answers but rather he would peer over his glasses at them in the manner of a patient but increasingly frustrated head teacher. Seated next to his interpreter and close confidant, Salim Lamrani, Bielsa gave a measured and careful answer to every question.

'I feel a deep responsibility to give the fans the answers that they expect from me.'

15

Michael Gill

Marcelo Bielsa

Derby County 1 v Leeds United 4

August 11th. 2018

Derby County

Carson, Wisdom, Bryson, Tomori, Keogh, Wilson (Jozefzoon 61), Mount (Bennett 75), Waghorn, Lawrence, Lowe, Ledley (Johnson 45).
Unused Substitutes: Roos, Forsyth, Marriott, Pearce.

Leeds United

Peacock – Farrell, Ayling, Cooper, Phillips, Beradi, Douglas, Klich (Shackleton 73), Alioski, Hernandez, Saiz (Baker 86), Roofe (Bamford 79). Unused Substitutes: Blackman, Roberts, Jansson, Harrison.

Referee: P Bankes

Attendance: 27,311

Former Chelsea and England star Frank Lampard OBE had been appointed as Manager of Derby about a month before Bielsa came to Leeds. He had been a fine player but this was his first managerial appointment. In its time honoured fashion, the British press had hyped the appointment up as if he was sure to be an instant success. They had even rebranded the club 'Frank Lampard's Derby' and the East Midlands Club were strongly fancied as a major contender for the Championship crown.

They received a rude awakening on this hot August afternoon as they were comprehensively picked apart by Bielsa's men.

Last season's strugglers seemed to have been transformed into a cohesive attacking force: Saiz fizzed and popped all over the pitch. KLICH (5) was composed and took the opening goal well. Seven minutes later, Derby edged themselves back into the game when LAWRENCE (12) hit a fine free kick. Bailey Peacock – Farrell seemed to be well positioned but failed to reach the shot.

United were not to be denied for long, however. Alioski crossed the ball with precision and ROOFE (21) restored their lead with a fine headed goal.

In the second half, the Whites kept up the pressure and were rewarded when Hernandez sent another defence – splitting cross in. It eluded Alioski but ROOFE (60) was on hand to turn smartly and stick the ball in the net.

ALIOSKI (64) added the icing to the cake, converting a Hernandez cross.

This was a great team performance and wonderful football to watch. The speed at which United moved the ball from defence to attack was stunning. They were equally impressive at tracking back on the few occasions when this was required of them. Having achieved 51% of the possession against Stoke, they now increased this to 53%. Put simply, Derby did not know what had hit them!

People were now starting to sit up and take notice: Maybe this coach was weaving some magic at Elland Road. As always with the English Press, the praise was excessive, just as excessive as the criticism would be as soon as they would get a chance to dish some of that out. Some of the self appointed experts had done a small amount of research on the Argentine.

'This is what happens with all of his teams. They start well and then burn out because he has killed their stamina by pushing too hard!'

Many of the Leeds fans, though delighted, kept their feet on the ground, remembering how well the Chritiansen side had started the previous season, only to fade after Christmas.

'It was maybe too much difference of the score. It was more clear in the

second half but in the first half we suffered some actions which could have allowed the rivals to score goals.'
Marcelo Bielsa

Leeds United 2 v Bolton Wanderers 1 (Carabao Cup)

August 14th 2018

Leeds United

Blackman, Shackleton, Ayling, Janssen, Phillips, Pearce, Harrison, Saiz (Alioski 68), Baker, Roberts, (Klich 68), Bamford (Roofe 80). Unused Substitutes: Huffer, DeBock, Beradi, Shaughnessy.

Bolton Wanderers

Matthews, Little, Vela, Oztumer, Donaldson (Noone 57) Hobbs, Wilson, O'Neil, Grounds (Taylor 74), Wildschutt, Hall (Magennis 65). Unused Substitutes: Alnwick, Beevers, Olkowski, Pritchard.

Referee: A Haines

Attendance: 19,617

Blackman, Bamford and Shackleton made their first starts for United and a very respectable crowd 0f 19,617 was interested in looking at the performance of all three of them, albeit for different reasons. Bamford, of course was the Whites most expensive signing since Robbie Fowler in 2001. Blackman was the Chelsea Loanee who had been expected to step straight into the team as goalkeeper. Shackleton was a prodigious talent from the academy that Bielsa had immediately spotted and elevated to the first team group.

None of the trio was to disappoint: BAMFORD (27) opened the scoring after nutmegging Jack Hobbs. He came close on several other occasions and was substituted by Roofe after 80 minutes to generous applause from the Faithful. Blackman and Shackleton both put in the full 90 minutes and gave solid performances.

SAIZ (35) added a second goal for Leeds. This was to be the mercurial Spaniard's last goal for the club.

In the second half, the Whites could and should have added to their tally but instead, they allowed Bolton to get back into the game when (OZTUMER 52) found the bottom left hand corner of the goal from the edge of the box.

Nevertheless, United dominated and held out for their third win in a row. It was clear that despite the eight changes in personnel, that the team stayed true to the high energy style and this was borne out by the possession statistics which showed United 57% to Bolton 43%.

'Even if the starters were new, they respected the style of the team. We had good balance and offensively we were good enough to win by more. But of course when it's 2-1 near the end, you get worried.'
Marcelo Bielsa.

Leeds United 2 v Rotherham United 0

August 18th 2018

Leeds United

Peacock – Farrell, Ayling, Cooper, Beradi, Phillips, Douglas, Klich (Jansson 90+1), Alioski, Saiz (Baker 80) Hernandez, Roofe (Bamford 86).
Unused Substitutes: Pearce, Harrison, Shackleton.

Rotherham United

Rodak, Vyner, Mattock, Vaulks, Ajayi, Wood (Vassall 76), Palmer (Manning 66), Taylor, Williams, Smith (Proctor 78), Raggett.
Unused Substitutes: Bilboe, Ball, Robertson, Newell.

Referee: R Jones

Attendance: 33,699

Rotherham came to Elland Road with the intention of 'spoiling the party.' In the first half, they were largely successful in this aim and even came close to scoring when Jon Taylor's fine shot hit the post. This was a rare foray on their part and they were generally content to sit back and absorb the pressure.

Leeds came close through Ayling, Klich and Beradi but had to retire at half time with no goals to show for their efforts.

The Millers finally cracked when (AYLING 49) headed the ball across the line. After a short delay, this fact was confirmed by goal line technology.

(ROOFE 71) added a second, finishing off a great run with a fine shot from a tight angle.

By this time, the Rotherham team were a spent force and showed their fatigue as Leeds sprayed the ball around at will. This was a solid win against a team with a different style to those previously encountered in the Championship. The possession ratio was a staggering: Leeds 73% Rotherham 27%. 'Bielsaball' was starting to take a hold.

Position in Championship Table After Match: 2nd.

'Unlike the first two games, the game today looked more like a Championship game.'
Marcelo Bielsa

Swansea City 2 v Leeds United 2

August 21st 2018

Swansea

Milder, Naughton, van der Hoorn, Rodon, Olsson (Assoro 83), Fulton, Fer (Carroll 74) Roberts, Celina, McKay (Montero 64), McBurnie.
Unused Substitutes: Benda, James, Grimes, Dhanda.

Leeds

Peacock – Farrell, Ayling, Shackleton, Beradi, Phillips (Baker

28), Douglas, Hernandez, Saiz, Klich, Alioski (Harrison 45) Roofe (Bamford 64).
Unused Substitutes: Blackman, Pearce, Shaughnessy, Rey.

Referee: A Davies

Attendance: 20,860

Liam Cooper injured his hamstring in the warm up allowing Jamie Shackleton to make his Championship debut. Unsurprisingly, eyebrows were raised about fans' favourite Pontus Janssen not being in the squad and the 'doom and gloom' merchants were already reaching for their cyanide pills.

Swansea took the lead through (MCBURNIE 24). The Leeds – born striker slipped the ball past Peacock - Farrell after McKay broke up a Leeds attack, finding Celina who put the Heckingbottom favourite through.

One of the standout players under Bielsa's reign so far was Kalvin Phillips who had proved to be a versatile performer. He was as comfortable playing in front of the centre backs or indeed as part of a back three. Nevertheless, Bielsa withdrew him on 28 minutes for tactical reasons, replacing him with Lewis Baker.

Just before half time, United equalised. ROOFE (40) slotted home an equaliser after great work from Jamie Shackleton.

Harrison and Bamford replaced Alioski and Roofe for the second half as it was clear that United were going to continue on the offensive.

Unfortunately, the persistent MCBURNIE (51) headed home an Olsson cross to give the Swans the lead and another twenty eight minutes elapsed before HERNANDEZ (79) helped Leeds draw level after good work from Patrick Bamford.

Both sides had their chances and this game proved to be United's sternest test under Bielsa.

Michael Gill

Position in Championship Table After Match: 1st

After we scored again at 2-2, we dominated the game but we could have won this game and we could have lost it too. It was a nice game to watch.
Marcelo Bielsa

Between the Railway Station and Carrow Road, Norwich City's ground is a Leisure and Shopping Precinct. Within this precinct is a Wetherspoons Pub which delights in the dramatic name: 'The Queen of Iceni.'

On previous visits to this fine city on match days, I have never managed to get served in this pub, owing to its enormous popularity. Usually there is a queue up to five deep at the bar and to relieve this, staff stand at the entrance with baskets full of plastic bottles of Carlsberg or something equally bland.

On this warm August day, armed with my Wetherspoons app, I bypassed the plastic bottle vendors and found a seat at the corner of a table. Within ten minutes I was served up with a Mixed Grill and an excellent pint of Shipyard. Pure Genius!

The reason I mention this is not as a tribute to Tim Martin and his excellent business but I need to say a bit about the eponymous 'Queen of Iceni'

According to history books, Boudicca was a Warrior Queen who led the Celtic Iceni Tribe. The tribe was based not far from Carrow Road. She was fearless and brave and initiated several revolts against the occupying forces of Rome.

Boudicca was unimpressed with her sneaky and devious husband and many of her wimpish warriors. A bloodthirsty lass alright and clearly no relation to Delia Smith!

Taking a leaf out of Boudicca's book, Delia and her fellow Directors hatched a cunning plan to emasculate members of the away teams who visited Carrow Road by painting the walls of the away dressing room a delicate shade of pink. It is rumoured that they had been advised in this course of action by a former Sports Psychologist who is now believed to be working in a PPI Call Centre.

Can you imagine Gaetano Beradi helping Luke Ayling to tie his topknot and admiring the luxuriance of his golden locks? No I can't either! Nice try Delia!

Norwich City 0 v Leeds United 3

August 25th 2018

Norwich City

Krul, Pinto, Hanley, Close, Lewis, Thompson (Stiepermann 81), Trybull, Pukki, Leitner, (Buenda 75), Hernandez, Rhodes, (Srbeny 81).
Unused Substitutes: Godfrey, Zimmerman.

Leeds United

Peacock – Farrell, Ayling, Jansson, Beradi, Phillips, Douglas, Hernandez (Harrison 79), Saiz (Baker 90), Klich, Alioski, Roofe (Bamford 77).
Unused Substitutes: Blackman, Pearce, Shaughnessy, Shackleton.

Referee: S Hooper.

Attendance: 25,944

United showed no ill effects from the Swansea game and didn't seem to be upset by the colour of the changing room wall. It took The Whites about fifteen minutes to get into their routine: After Krul parried away Alioski's header. KLICH (21) grabbed his third goal of the season and Leeds turned on the power. ALIOSKI (26) hit a fine strike from the left and the Leeds team were irrepressible.

For another short spell at the beginning of the second half, United were on the back foot but they held firm with sound performances from Beradi and Jansson.

Michael Gill

However, Norwich soon faded away and when HERNANDEZ (67) scored with a fine solo effort, the game was all but over. United were back in their groove and Norwich were literally give the run around.

Only wasteful finishing from Saiz and Bamford prevented the match from becoming a massacre.

In his short tenure Bielsa has made this team believe in themselves.

As I left the ground, I heard several Norwich fans muttering about the manager; Daniel Farke. Their wishes to have him removed would not have been a good idea!

Position in Championship Table After Match: 1st.

'I think that he (Hernandez) can make me a better Head Coach!'

Marcelo Bielsa. (When asked if he could make Pablo Hernandez a better player).

Leeds United 0 Preston North End 2 (Carabao Cup)

August 28th 2018

Leeds United

Blackman, Pearce, Shaughnessy (Klich 45) Jansson, Shackleton (Saiz 45), Baker, Phillips, Harrison, Dallas, Roberts (Alioski 60), Bamford.
Unused Substitiutes: Huffer, Douglas, Roofe.

Preston North End

Maxwell, Fisher, Earl, Davies, Moult (Nmecha 75), Harrop, Johnson (Pearson71), Storey, Ledson, Barker (Browne 72), Barkhuizen.
Unused Substitutes: Rudd, Hughes, Huntington, Burke.

Referee: T Harrington

Attendance: 18,652

24

United got off to a bad start in this game and never really recovered. Pontus Jansson brought down Louis Moult in the box after less than a minute and JOHNSON (2) Converted a penalty, sending Jamal Blackman the wrong way.

Leeds went close several times but could not get the ball in the net. On 29 minutes, Ryan Ledson was given a straight red card for a terrible two footed tackle on Louis Baker.

Against the run of play, Preston went two up when BARKER (45+1) scored a fine solo effort as a result of a counter attack.

The second half followed a similar pattern with United battering away without reward as Preston honed their time – wasting skills to perfection. It became clear after the first hour that this was not going to be United's night as Preston became the first team to prevent them from scoring.

'They only needed four chances to score two goals. We had twelve chances and couldn't score any. My conclusion is we didn't play well but I don't think the result should have been a defeat for us.'
Marcelo Bielsa

Leeds United 0 v Middlesbrough 0

August 31st 2018

Leeds United

Peacock – Farrell, Ayling, Beradi (Jansson 88), Cooper, Phillips, Douglas, Klich, Harrison (Dallas 90+2), Alioski, Saiz, Roofe (Bamford 90).
Substitutes not used: Blackman, Roberts, Pearce, Baker.

Middlesbrough

Randolph, Friend, Ayala, Shotton, Clayton, Assombalonga, Howson, Downing, Fry, Flint, Besic. Substitutes not used: Dimi, Leadbitter, Braithwaite, Hugill, McQueen, McNair, Wing.

Referee: T Robinson

Attendance: 35,417

What happens when the irresistible force meets the immovable object? Nothing in this case.

Near neighbours Middlesbrough were greeted by a noisy but nervous Elland Road crowd. The mood was not improved by the news that Pablo Hernandez was not fit to play.

The other big selection decision was to replace fans favourite Pontus Jansson with returning captain, Liam Cooper. This decision was totally vindicated as Cooper had a fine game. Liam's central partner, Gaetano Beradi had another good game which only came to an end when he took a heavy knock.

This was not only a game of contrasting styles but a tale of two defences. In the end, honours were even and in some ways another hurdle was jumped by United who proved that they can defend with the best of them. Nevertheless, it was tempting to think that had Pablo Hernandez been available, United might have achieved a narrow win.

Position in Championship Table After Match: 1st.

'It is a fair result. It was very hard to build our game. In spite of this we could have had four or five attempts on their goal.'
Marcelo Bielsa

CHAPTER 3

September 2018 – The International Break and The First Defeat

Michael Gill

September brought the first International Break. All International breaks are agony for football fans but the first one of the season is the worst, for having enjoyed their drug of choice for a whole month they now have it snatched away from them.

To ease the pain, I went to watch Gillingham lose 1-0 at home to Wimbledon in an effort to knock another ground off in my quest to visit all 92 of them. Few things were memorable about this trip apart from the Gill's big raw boned striker; Tom Eaves and the worst fish and chips that I have ever tasted. Eaves didn't score on this occasion but he has since proved to be a handy lad at cracking goals in almost at will.

Kemar Roofe had been named Championship Player of the Month for August and unsurprisingly he was joined by Marcelo Bielsa as Manager of the Month.

Although Bielsa accepted the award with good grace, he refused to be photographed with it as he felt that it was premature to be receiving such an award. He is said to have given the trophy to Victor Orta to put away in a cupboard until such time as the club's objectives for the season had been met.

United's return to the action was in that unattractive corner of South East London known as Bermondsey. Apart from Del Boy, Rodney and Tommy Steele, the area has little to recommend it. The self–styled 'family club of the year:' Millwall call this quaint backwater their home. I wonder if teaching eight year old children how to do throat – slitting gestures is part of the curriculum that is taught by the family club of the year or whether this is just a personal initiative.

I enjoyed a couple of pre – match pints in the 'Market Porter' before disappearing into Borough Market to find the Salt Beef Sandwich stall. Then I walked past the Shard and into London Bridge Station, avoiding the scuffles before getting into the train to travel one stop to South Bermondsey and the segregated walkways to the New Den.

This has not been a happy hunting ground for United in recent years. Some of the previous managers didn't help with their recitation of the usual platitudes: 'It's always a difficult place to come to, Brian.' Or 'It's always an intimidating atmosphere at the Den.' etc. etc.

Millwall rarely fill their small stadium and if, as they claim, the knuckle - dragging Neathandral fans are in the minority, then what is there to worry about?

Millwall 1 v Leeds United 1

September 15th 2018

Millwall

Amos, McLaughlin, Meredith, Cooper, Williams, Wallace, Gregory (Elliott 87) Morison (Bradshaw 70), O'Brien, Wallace, Leonard. Unused Substitutes: Skalak, Webster, Tunnicliffe, Martin, Romeo.

Leeds United

Peacock – Farrell, Ayling, Cooper, Phillips (Forshaw 74) Jansson, Douglas, Klich (Baker 71) Harrison, Alioski Saiz, Roberts (Dallas 68) Unused Substitutes: Blackman, Pearce, Edmonson, Clarke.

Referee: C Kavanagh

Attendance: 17,195

Leeds had some tough news on the injury front before this match. The club announced that Pablo Hernandez was likely to be out for four to five weeks. To make matters worse, big money signing Patrick Bamford had sustained a serious injury in an under 23 game. (Posterior Cruciate Ligament) and was likely to be out for the next four months. To make matters worse, in – form striker Kemar Roofe was likely to be out for two to three weeks with a calf injury. This trio was joined by Gaetano Beradi who would be out for approximately three weeks with the knee injury he sustained against Middlesbrough.

The more negative supporters pointed at the small squad while some of the pundits hinted that these injuries had been caused by the intensity of Bielsa's training methods, although the facts did not bear this out. Ironically, these circumstances gave last season's centre back pairing of Cooper and Jansson the opportunity to start together for the first time this season.

The Whites might not have won this game but they laid a ghost.

In the end, a draw was probably a fair result but it felt like a win. United played their usual game but could not break the Millwall defence down and honours were even at halftime despite the fact that both Roberts and Alioski came very close to scoring.

Ten minutes after the break, (WALLACE (56) put the home side ahead with a scrambled effort.

United kept going as Millwall ran the clock down. A fracas developed between the two benches as Millwall tried to prevent Leeds from getting the ball back into play. Just when it seemed that the Whites would have to accept an undeserved defeat, HARRISON (89) hit a sweet strike from the edge of the box to equalise and transport the Leeds fans to Disneyland.

Ever the sportsman, Millwall's manager Neil Harris described United's celebrations as 'a disgrace to British football.' Bielsa later apologised and Harris appeared to accept his apology. The Millwall Boss forgot about this a couple of days later and continued his xenophobic bellyaching in the South London Mercury and Press

The goal had come as a result of United's high pressing game and was thoroughly deserved.
Six frantic minutes of added time followed as the home side threw everything at their visitors.

This was a moral victory for United who remained at the top of the Championship table.

Position in Championship Table After Match: 1st.

'I am responsible for this situation. I take responsibility because I am in football longer than my colleague (Neil Harris). I have to understand that the circumstances that you have during a game, you don't have to take them as they are. If you win or lose, it means a lot to us and sometimes we behave in a kind of way just after we lament our behaviour.'
Marcelo Bielsa

Michael Gill

Leeds United 3 v Preston North End 0

September 18th 2018

Leeds United

Peacock – Farrell, Ayling, Cooper, Jansson, Phillips, Douglas, Klich (Forshaw 88), Alioski, Harrison, Saiz, (Baker 90), Roberts, (Dallas 86).
Unused Substitutes: Blackman, Forshaw, Pearce, Edmonson, Clarke.

Preston North End

Rudd, Fisher, Earl, Clarke, Davies, Robinson, Browne (Gallagher 79), Moult (Nmecha 79), Harrop (Barker 71), Johnson, Barkhuizen.
Unused Substitutes: Maxwell, Hughes, Burke, Huntington.

Referee: G Eltringham

Attendance: 27,729

Still without Roofe and Bamford, Tyler Roberts led the line and was hoping to convert some chances this time after a couple of near misses at Millwall.

Preston started in a lively fashion but they were not as fast off the blocks as they had been in the Carabaou Cup.

However, once United settled into the game, they started to dominate. Klich came close after good work from Jack Harrison. Ayling provided Roberts with another chance which drew a good save from Rudd. Barry Douglas took a finely measured corner and COOPER (37) scored with a diving header.

United continued to give Preston problems and should have gone into the second half with a couple more goals under their belts.

It was long after the hour when ROBERTS (74) spotted Rudd off his lie and lobbed the ball over his head for the second goal. Eight minutes later, the likeable youngster doubled his tally. Saiz found Klich who crossed the ball for ROBERTS (82) to head home and kill off any resistance from Preston.

Position in Championship Table After Match: 1st.

'Tyler Roberts thought he had to play as a number nine and in the game against Millwall he had four chances to score. Today he scores two goals so it's an interesting performance. He's a very young player and I'm very happy for him. He deserves it.'
Marcelo Bielsa

Leeds United 1 v Birmingham City 2

22nd September 2018

Leeds United

Peacock – Farrell, Ayling (Dallas 34), Cooper, Phillips, Jansson, Douglas (Edmonson 71) Klich (Forshaw 72) Alioski, Saiz, Roberts.
Unused Substitutes: Blackman, Pearce, Baker, Shackleton.

Birmingham

Camp, Pederson, Colin, Adams, Jutkiewicz (Bogle 82), Dean, Maghoma, Gardner (Kieftenbeld 58), Jota (Harding 88), Morrison, Lakin.
Unused Substitutes: Trueman, Roberts, Mahoney, Solomon – Otabor.

Referee P Bankes.

Attendance: 34,800

The first Championship defeat had to come some time and there was a strange feeling of inevitability about it when ADAMS (2) opened the scoring. Things got worse twenty one minutes later when ADAMS (29) whacked in his second goal. The normally shot – shy team had found themselves two nil up away from home for the first time since they had led by a similar margin before throwing the lead away at Nottingham Forest.

One thing that former Leeds Boss Gary Monk's side were good at though was shutting up shop. This they did with frustrating efficiency.

It was only in the final stages of the game that United posed any counter attacking threat. ALIOSKI (85) pulled one back and even with eight minutes added on for Birmingham's outrageous time wasting, United could not find an equaliser.

The fans awaited 'El Loco's reaction to his first Championship defeat.

Position in Championship Table After Match: 1st.

'I don't have any complaints against the Referee. The situation he had to resolve was the one we saw and he used the rules to solve them so we have nothing to say against him.'
Marcelo Bielsa

Sheffield Wednesday 1 v Leeds United 1

September 28th 2018

Sheffield Wednesday

Dawson, Pelupessy, Fletcher (Nuhiu 77), Bannan, Thorniley, Lees, Reach, Baker (Palmer 59), Hector, Penney, Forestieri (Joao 81). Unused Substitutes:Wildsmith, Onoma, Rice, Preston.

Leeds

Peacock – Farrell, Ayling, Cooper, Phillips, Jansson, Douglas, Klich, Alioski, Harrison, Saiz (Forshaw (90), Roberts. Unused Substitutes: Blackman, Dallas, Pearce, Baker, Shackleton, Clarke.

Referee: R Jones

Attendance:26,717

Prior to this game, there was the usual anticipation, excitement and more than a little anxiety. Leeds had just suffered their first defeat at home. Had Bielsa's bubble burst? The answer was clearly 'No.' The Whites put on such a dominant performance that it made a mockery of the eventual result.

United were in a different league to their near neighbours when it came to energy commitment and class.

REACH (45) put Wednesday in front with a fine looking goal. Had he not scored goals like this before, you would have been tempted to say that he lashed a speculative volley which miraculously found the net.

KLICH (54) equalised with a screamer of his own which was over-due when looking at the high standards that the Polish midfielder had set himself. Try as they might, United could not conjure up a winner.

The 'glass half empty' brigade would rue the missed chances but to have a chance in the first place, you must create one and the Whites created plenty of chances.

Position in Championship Table After Match: 1st.

'I'm truly disappointed. I don't like to judge the performance of the opponent but the fact that we had twenty five chances to score talks about what we deserved.'
Marcelo Bielsa

CHAPTER 4

October 2018 – Swings and Roundabouts.

Hull City 0 v Leeds United 1

October 2nd 2018

Hull City

Marshall, Lichaj, Burke, Grosicki (Dicko 65), Irvine (Stewart 28), Kane, Bowen, Henricksen, Kingsley, Martin (Campbell 64), El-phick.
Unused Substitutes: Batty, Keane, Curry, McKenzie.

Leeds United

Peacock – Farrell, Ayling, Cooper, Jansson, Phillips, Douglas (Shackleton 82) Klich, Harrison (Dallas 74) Alioski, Saiz (Forshaw 74) Roberts.
Unused Substitutes: Blackman, Pearce, Baker, Clarke.

Referee: D Bond

Attendance: 13,798

New Manager Nigel Adkins was just starting to get to grips with under – achieving Hull City. The Tigers had managed to draw with high – flying Middlesbrough at the weekend and were expected to put up a strong challenge to frustrate the Whites.

In the first half, Roberts, Saiz, Alioski, Klich, Cooper and Douglas all came close for United but the Tigers were in no mood to give anything away.

It took a spectacular goal from ROBERTS (51) to give United the lead. The youngster drifted into space twenty five yards out from goal before hitting a perfect shot into the left hand corner.

Position in Championship Table After Match: 1st.

'We were not efficient enough. When there is just a one goal difference there is always the possibility of scoring a goal. This made the game more complicated than it was. Until the last ten minutes, we controlled the game, controlled possession, controlled the field.'
Marcelo Bielsa

Leeds United 1 v Brentford 1

6th October 2018

Leeds United

Peacock – Farrell, Ayling, Dallas (Clarke 70), Cooper, Jansson, Phillips, Klich (Forshaw 63), Alioski, Harrison, Saiz (Baker 76), Roberts.
Unused Substitutes: Blackman, Pearce, Shackleton, Edmonson.

Brentford

Daniels, Odubajo (Barbet 76), Mepham, Canos (Benrahma 77), Yennaris, Maupay, Watkins (Judge 84), Mokotjo, Sawyers, Dalsgaard, Konsa.
Unused Substitutes: Bentley, MacLeod, McEachran, Jeanvier.

Referee: J. Simpson

Attendance: 31,880

Another frustrating afternoon at Elland Road saw The Whites draw with Brentford and slip to third place. The unrelenting nature of the Championship meant that Sheffield United and West Brom nudged past Leeds as the upcoming International Break would give everybody a chance for a 'breather.'

It would also give the referee, Mr. Simpson an opportunity to reflect on the consequences of his decision making.

He penalised Bailey Peacock – Farrell after he had made a fine reaction save with his feet. Ollie Watkins was already falling as he dived spectacularly over the keeper's outstretched arms. Bailey is a big lad and that meant that Watkins was about eight feet away from the ball when the alleged incident occurred.

MAUPAY (62) converted the resultant penalty, to put United up against it.

As United became more desperate, JANSSON (88) headed home the equaliser from an Alioski free kick to rescue a point.

Simpson further angered the Elland Road crowd as he sent Ayling off for a second bookable offence.

Despite the controversy a draw was probably a fair result.

Position in Championship Table After Match: 3rd.

'I think it is a fair result. We could have won the game and we could have lost the game but it wouldn't be fair to say that we were close to winning the game. That wasn't the case.'
Marcelo Bielsa

Blackburn Rovers 2 v Leeds United 1

Blackburn Rovers

Raya, Reed (Conway 69) Smallwood (Rodwell 58) Armstrong, Graham (Brereton 63) Mulgrew, Bell, Dack, Lenihan, Evans, Bennett.
Unused Substitutes: Leutwiler, Williams, Rothwell, Palmer.

Leeds United

Peacock – Farrell, Beradi (Shackleton 86),Cooper, Jansson, Dallas (Clarke 76), Phillips, Klich, Alioski, Saiz, Roofe (Hernandez (71), Roberts.
Unused Substitutes: Blackman, Forshaw, Pearce, Baker.

Referee: D England

Attendance: 20,029

East Lancashire is the home of good meat pies and no visit to Blackburn is complete without calling in at one of my favourite Pie Shops. For once it had to be post – match as the match had an early kick off thanks to our friends at Sky Sports. Still this didn't deter nearly eight thousand Leeds fans from making their trip across the Pennines. The Leeds contingent took up almost 40% of the total attendance. They were in good voice and expecting three points. Beradi and Roofe were back in the team and Hernandez was on the bench. Things were looking good.

However, the sad – faced Tony Mowbray is a seasoned Championship manager and he had a few tricks up his sleeve.

United started badly again. They conceded two corners straight away and from the second one GRAHAM (2) put Rovers ahead.

Bailey Peacock – Farrell made good saves from Dack and Smallwood.

Leeds had started slowly but Dallas came close and they were just into stoppage time when KLICH (45+ 1) scored his fifth goal of the season. Saiz had floated in a defence – splitting cross to Beradi who squared the ball to the Pole for an easy finish. The Leeds contingent went crazy and rocked the ground with their noise.

In the second half, United fell for another sucker punch set piece after LENIHAN (70) headed home Conway's corner.

Leeds pushed hard but without reward and although the pie was excellent, it didn't taste as good as they usually do.

Position in Championship Table After Match: 4th.

'Maybe a draw would have reflected better what happened during the game. We played better when the opponent was winning and this is the defect.'
Marcelo Bielsa

Leeds United 2 v Ipswich Town 0

24th October 2018

Leeds United

Peacock – Farrell, Ayling, Cooper, Beradi (Dallas 27), Alioski, Phillips, Klich, Harrison (Pearce 57), Saiz (Forshaw 57), Hernandez, Roofe.
Unused Substitutes: Blackman, Roberts, Baker, Clarke.

Ipswich Town: Bialkowski, Knudsen, Chambers, Pennington, Skuse (Chalobah 85), Jackson, Nolan, Spence, Sears (Edwards 76), Downes, Edun (Ward 82).

Unused Substitutes: Gerken, Donacien, Dozell.

Referee C Pawson

Attendance: 29,082

For six years, Mick McCarthy had managed Ipswich Town on a shoestring budget before being sacked by the 'ambitious' board after pressure from the fan base. Mick did not do himself too many favours by describing some of the home fans as 'numb-skulls' and by the time he left he had probably had enough anyway. McCarthy was a Barnsley lad and an avowed Leeds fan and was adjudged by most people to have done a first class job at the East Anglian Club. Whenever a managerial vacancy appeared at Leeds, his name was also mentioned. He was replaced by Paul Hurst who had acquitted himself well at Shrewsbury town but before this match had only achieved one Championship win out of thirteen matches.

This time, Pablo Hernandez was in the starting line up as Leeds tried to tap into his creative talents and it wasn't too long before he was on hand to float a beautiful cross to ROOFE (22) who made no mistake in rising to the occasion to head home his fifth of the season. Later in the first half, Gaetano Beradi had to withdraw with a hamstring tendon rupture which would keep him out until the following March.

In the second half, Leeds continued to pepper the Ipswich goal with shots from all angles until Hernandez crossed to COOPER (66) who hit a fine shot from the edge of the area into the bottom corner of the Ipswich net.

This was a routine game which United were expected to win and they did not disappoint.

One win out of thirteen became one win out of fourteen and Paul Hurst was fired the following day.

Position in Championship Table After Match: 1ˢᵗ.

41

Michael Gill

'I am very happy to work with this team, with this club, in this country and for these fans but the only way to thank all the people who believed in me is to get a more important win at the end of the season. It's always dangerous when you get expressions of gratitude in the middle of the season, not at the end of the season. The gratitude is my answer to the praise and these praises only last if we have lasting victories. There's nothing more important than to feel loved. To deserve the praise we need to do a lot more.'
Marcelo Bielsa

Leeds United 1 v Nottingham Forest 1

27ᵗʰ October 2018

Leeds United

Peacock – Farrell, Ayling (Pearce 25), (Clarke 65), Cooper, Jansson, Dallas, Phillips (Saiz 65), Klich, Forshaw, Alioski, Hernandez, Roofe.
Unused Substitutes: Blackman, Roberts, Baker, Shackleton.

Nottingham Forest

Pantilimon, Figueiredo, Fox (Dawson 51), Guedioura, Colback, Grabban, Carvalho, Cash (Diaz 87), Robinson, Lolley (Osborn 69), Darikwa.
Unused Substitutes: Steel, Soudani, Watson, Janko.

Referee: G Eltringham

Attendance: 34,308

Once again, United conceded an early set piece when ROBINSON (11) headed home Joe Lolly's well struck corner.

Hernandez and Roofe both came close before United's injury hoodoo struck again. Ayling left the field with a serious knee injury and was replaced by Tom Pearce. United continued to press for the equaliser, roared on by the near capacity crowd. Forshaw came closest with a 25 yard drive which beat Pantillimon only to pass by the wrong side of his post.

In the second half, Clarke and Saiz were introduced as the Whites continued to ramp up the pressure. United finally levelled the score when Saiz crossed the ball to Dallas. The Irishman switched the ball to Klich who sent it across the goal mouth. ROOFE (82) was on 'hand' to bundle the ball into the back of the net as the Kop erupted. Pantillimon ran over to the referee, pointing to his hand. Surrounded by Forest players, Mr Eltringham consulted his linesman before confirming that the goal stood.

I was stood directly opposite Roofe in North East Lower and the goal looked fine to me but my companion received a text from someone who was watching the game on Sky TV. The viewer confirmed that Kemar had, indeed struck the ball with his hand on the way in. Such are the miracles of modern science but it is nice to get a bit of luck sometimes.

Leeds nearly wrapped it up in the dying minutes when Alioski crossed the ball to Hernandez who cheekily back heeled it and nearly scored.

Phillips was booked for Leeds and Grabban, Colback, Carvalho and Dias for Forest in a brutal encounter. A draw was probably a fair result given United's dominance and the way in which they equalised.

Position in Championship Table After Match: 2nd.

'A draw is not enough to give the reward the team deserved. But I have admiration for the noble character of the opponent. They might have wasted time in an exaggerated manner but every time they recovered the ball, they tried to play. The features of the opponent give merit to our performance but I don't celebrate a draw because for me when we play at home with 35,000 fans, a draw is not good enough. Our performance was good. The opponent is one of the good teams in the Championship. In my opinion it was a beautiful game.'
Marcelo Bielsa

CHAPTER 5

*November 2018 - Adver-
sity and Recovery*

Wigan 1 v Leeds United 2

4th. November 2018

Wigan Athletic

Walton, James, Kipre, Burn ,Robinson, Byrne, Gibson (Vaughan 85), Morsy, Naismith (Da Silva Lopes 70), Widass, Garner (McManaman 64).
Unused Substitutes: MacDonald, Dunkley, Jones, Evans.

Leeds United

Peacock – Farrell, Cooper, Jansson, Phillips, Dallas, Douglas, Klich (Shackleton (90+1), Forshaw, Roofe, Hernandez, Alioski.
Unused Substitutes: Blackman, Baker, Harrison, Roberts, Clarke, Saiz.

Referee: A Davies

Attendance: 14,799

This game witnessed the final involvement of the Whelan family with the Wigan after 23 years. Former player and hard nosed Lancashire businessman Dave Whelan had built the club up, developed the stadium and took them from the third tier to the Premier League. This was a remarkable achievement and he was probably one of the last of the old style Club Chairmen. Ironically Leeds were the visitors in March 2015 when Dave resigned as Chairman and on that occasion, fans arriving early were treated to a long, rambling and almost incoherent speech in which he sang his own praises.

United entered this latest game to face a team which had recently been promoted from League One. Unfortunately the Latics were now fighting against relegation. The one thing that was keeping them afloat was their home form. Incredibly, they had not lost a game at the JJB since the previous February.

Wigan got off to a lively if somewhat fortunate start. Liam Cooper was very unlucky to concede a free kick after being fouled himself. JAMES (6) buried the free kick and the 'set piece curse' had manifested itself again.

Within a few minutes, Barry Douglas sent Mateus Klich away with a defence – splitting pass, the Polish international picked out HERNANDEZ (9) who side footed the ball into the net. After that, there was only one team in it.

United's second goal came from a horrendous defensive error. ROOFE (46) was on hand to tap the ball into the net.

The scoreline barely did the Whites justice as they had bossed this game from the equaliser onwards. Wigan were brushed aside with some pulsating football and the Whites seemed to have recovered some of the mastery which they had practiced earlier in the season.

What really defined this match was United's total dominance. From front to back, they worked as a super – efficient unit and were completely unstoppable.

Position in Championship Table After Match: 1st.

'When we have possession it increases our self esteem because one of our goals is to prevent the opponent the ball. If we can prevent the opponent from making too many passes and recover the ball from the third or fourth pass, we feel safer and the opponent loses confidence.'
Marcelo Bielsa

West Bromwich Albion 4 v Leeds United 1

10th November 2018

West Bromwich Albion

Johnstone, Gibbs (Mears 88), Robson – Kanu (Gayle 79), Morrison, Livermore, Phillips (Harper 90+2), Barnes, Rodrigues, Adarabioyo, Dawson, Hegazi.
Unused Substitutes: Myhill, Barry, Hoolahan, Sako.

Leeds United

Peacock – Farrell, Dallas, Jansson, Cooper, Douglas (Harrison 63), Phillips, Klich (Saiz 78), Forshaw, Hernandez, Alioski, Roofe (Roberts 66).

Unused Substitutes: Blackman, Baker, Davis, Shackleton.

Referee: L Mason

Attendance:25,661

Honours were fairly even in the first half as the Baggies sat back and relied on counter attacks. Forshaw, Klich and Roofe all had good efforts denied them and West Brom came close through Matt Phillips, Adarabioyo, Robson – Kanu and Rodriguez.

The deadlock was finally broken when Rodriguez sent ROBSON – KANU (51) away to plant the ball into the bottom right hand corner.

The ineffective Roofe was substituted by Tyler Roberts but Leeds could not take advantage of their dominant possession.

 PHILLIPS (67) scored with a shot from the edge of the box to the bottom left hand corner.

As the clock ran down it was clear that desperate measures were called for if United were to make anything of this game. As the game entered the final fifteen minutes, Bielsa threw his remaining chips across the green baize and replaced Douglas and Klich with Saiz and Harrison.

Sadly, it wasn't United's night and the prodigious BARNES (82) and substitute GAYLE (83) added to United's misery.

Hernandez (90+2) netted a goal which would be more accurately described as an irrelevance rather than a consolation.

The fact that Albion could afford to keep a player like Dwight Gayle on the bench spoke volumes for their fire power. Just like Stoke and Swansea, they were running a Premier League squad and so far they were performing much better than either of their fellow relegation partners.

Even if you forget about the first half and the fact that Bielsa threw caution to the wind at the final stages of the game, this was still the most comprehensive defeat that United had suffered all season.

Position in Championship Table After Match: 3rd.

'We knew before playing this game that the best aspect of the opponent was their offensive players. We knew that to use their skills they needed big spaces and they found big spaces to attack. I feel responsible for this loss. The problems and the solutions are always collective.'
Marcelo Bielsa

United had fourteen days to reflect on this heavy defeat as they went into the International Break. Their next opponents were Bristol City, a team that was once again punching above their weight. They were managed by Lee Johnson who had been linked with the manager's job at Leeds before they appointed Garry Monk. It was probably a lucky escape for him as even small setbacks would not have been tolerated by Massimo Cellino.

Leeds United 2 v Bristol City 0

November 24th. 2018

Leeds United

Huffer, Dallas, Halme (Saiz 74), Cooper, Douglas, Phillips, Forshaw, Klich (Baker 82), Hernandez, Alioski (Harrison 61), Roofe.
Unused Substitutes: Miazek, Davis, Shackleton, Clark.

Bristol City

Maenpaa, Hunt, Kalas, Webster, Kelly, Eliasson (Walsh 62), Pack, Brownhill, Adelakun (Diedhiou 62), Patterson (Eisa 78), Weimann.
Unused Substitutes: Pisano, DaSilva, Baker, O'Leary.

Referee: S Duncan

Attendance: 34,333

Second choice goalkeeper; Jemal Blackman had broken his leg in a development squad match a few days before this game. Despite this, Bielsa informed Bailey Peacock – Farrell that it had been his intention to play Blackman against Bristol City. We will never know what effect that this would have had on the youngster because he had picked up an injury himself in training and was unfit for selection.

United handed debuts to goalkeeper Will Huffer and central defender Aapo Halme as their defensive selection problems deepened.

The first half was a dour affair with both sides sounding each other out.

Almost an hour had elapsed before United came to life. Josh Brownhill had been sent off and this seemed to launch Leeds into action. Buoyed by the introduction of Harrison and Saiz, the Whites started to batter the Bristol goal. After the hour Pablo Hernandez set up ROOFE (67) with a finely weighted pass.

HERNANDEZ (86) scored one himself to wrap the game up, heading home a nice cross from Saiz.

Both debutantes fitted into the team seamlessly, looking as though they played at this level every week. The pragmatic way in which Bielsa introduced them must surely have contributed to their confidence.

Lee Johnson felt that Leeds were lucky to win and couldn't accept the reverse with good grace, saying that Leeds did not deserve their victory. In his polite, considered way, Marcelo had different views:

Position in Championship Table After Match: 3rd.

'As far as I know I don't remember anything of note that they created. It was a very comfortable debut for our goalkeeper today. When I watch the game again, I will take into account this point of view that we didn't deserve the result. That we played with one player more made it

easy for us but that wasn't the only reason we won. We did not domin-
ate the end of the first half or the start of the second half but we were
dominant from that point on.'
Marcelo Bielsa

Leeds United 1 v Reading 0

27th November 2018

Leeds United

Peacock – Farrell, Dallas, Cooper, Phillips, Douglas, Klich
(Shackleton 73), Forshaw, Baker (Saiz 45), Hernandez, Alioski
(Clarke 45), Roofe.
Unused Substitutes: Huffer, Roberts, Harrison, Halme.

Reading

Jaakkola, Gunter,Yiadom, Moore, Bacuna, Swift (McCleary 61),
Llori, Meite (Sims70), Rinomhota, Kelly (Mc Nulty 77), Loader.
Unused substitutes: Walker, O'Shea, Aluko, Blackett.

Referee: M Dean

Attendance 27,806

Bailey Peacock – Farrell returned to the side but Pontus Jansson
was still nursing his injury. United started in a lively fashion.
Pablo Hernandez found Barry Douglas at the far post only for the
former Wolves man to head wide. At the other end, Peacock –
Farrell tipped Bacuna's lobbed free kick over the bar. The young
keeper seemed to be showing no lack of confidence after the recent events.

Just before half time, Alioski went down in the box but was
booked for alleged simulation by Referee Mike Dean.

In the second half, Barry Douglas delivered a teasing cross from
the left, Roofe whacked it towards the target but it was blocked
by Reading's keeper Jaakkola who could only turn it into the path
of DALLAS (60) who made no mistake with the simple task of put-

ting it away.

Both goalkeepers were tested as the game drew to its conclusion. One minute from the end of normal time, Douglas felled Sims in the Leeds penalty box and the referee unhesitatingly pointed to the spot. Once again, the Whites were rueing missed chances as it looked as though they were going to have to be satisfied with one point.

McNulty stepped up to take the kick but he was denied by a fine save from Bailey Peacock – Farrell who was mobbed by his team mates to the tumultuous roar of the Elland Road crowd.

The Whites saw the stoppage time out and were able to chalk up back to back victories.

Position in Championship Table After Match: 2nd.

'Our behaviour had ups and downs, we were not all that regular. But generally speaking, we deserved to win.'
Marcelo Bielsa

CHAPTER 6

*December 2018 - Festive Frolics
and a Party Pooper*

Sheffield United 0 v Leeds United 1

December 1st 2018

Sheffield United

Henderson, Baldock, Stevens (Johnson 84), Fleck, O'Connell, Basham, Sharp, Egan, Norwood, McGoldrick, Duffy (Washington 62).
Unused Substitutes: Lundstram, Coutts, Shearman, Moore, Cranie.

Leeds United

Peacock – Farrell, Dallas, Cooper (Halme 21), Jansson, Douglas, Phillips, Forshaw, Klich, Hernandez (Shackleton 90), Alioski (Clarke 45), Roofe.
Unused Substitutes: Huffer, Saiz, Harrison, Baker.

Referee: O Langford

Attendance: 25,794

Twenty six years ago was the last time that the Whites had won at Bramall Lane. On that occasion, they beat the Blades 3-2 to clinch the old First Division Championship which remains their last major honour.

This game was not as important as that but was momentous nonetheless, as the Blades were pushing hard for promotion glory themselves.

The home team started on the front foot but after half an hour or so, Leeds edged themselves into the game. This was despite the fact that they had lost their captain Liam Cooper to injury after only 21 minutes.

By half time, Leeds were beginning to look more assertive and Aapo Halme slipped into Cooper's place as if it was the most natural thing in the world.

Young Jack Clarke joined the party for the second half and it was Clarke who pursued John Egan's over hit back pass. Stranded in the corner of the field, Goalkeeper Henderson seemed to have lots of time to reach the ball and kick it into touch. Instead, he al-

53

Michael Gill

lowed the Leeds man to dispossess him and pass the ball to HER-NANDEZ (82) who side footed the ball into an empty net.

This had been a very close game with the Whites achieving less than 50% possession for the first time in the season.

This result was a triumph over adversity, history and terrible refereeing.

Position in Championship Table After Match: 2nd.

'There was a moment, very important for me. My colleague, Pablo Quiroga told me to switch the position between Kemar Roofe and Pablo Hernandez and from that moment on, the play of the team improved. If the final result had been a draw, we couldn't say it had been an unfair result.'
Marcelo Bielsa

Leeds United 2 Queens Park Rangers 1

December 8th 2018

Leeds United

Peacock – Farrell, Shackleton, Phillips, Jansson, Douglas, Klich, Forshaw, Saiz (Halme 81), Alioski, Hernandez (Clarke 86), Roofe. Unused Substitutes: Huffer, Bamford, Harrison, Baker, Davis.

Queens Park Rangers

Lumley, Bidwell,Cameron, (Scowen 45), Freeman, Eze (Smith 78), Luongo, Rangel, Wszolek (Osayi – Samuel 73), Wells, Lynch,Leistner.
Unused Substitutes: Ingram, Furlong, Cousins, Hemed.

Referee P Bankes

Attendance: 33,781

Liam Cooper's enforced absence continued but Patrick Bamford was on the bench. He had not been expected to return from injury until January and although he didn't play, his presence was most welcome.

This game was never going to be an easy one but when Pontus Jansson headed the ball into the path of WELLS (26) it was clear that the Whites had given themselves another steep hill to climb.

United had started brightly enough but they seemed to falter a bit after the setback. Chance after chance went begging before ROOFE (45+3) put them level in the last action of the first half.

United started like a house on fire and were awarded their first penalty of the season. ROOFE (53) tucked it away safely after a brief conversation with captain for the day Pablo Hernandez.

Somehow, the Whites found themselves under the cosh again but held on for a nervous and nail biting finish. Nevertheless, it was their fourth win in a row.

Position in Championship Table After Match: 2nd.

'At the end of the game, Queens Park Rangers dominated the game but through different paths. At the end of the first half, we should have dominated and at the end of the second half we only had the option to adapt to the kind of play the opponent proposed.'
Marcelo Bielsa

On a horrible day, I parked my car at St Joseph's School on Chorley New Road and found an overgrown alleyway which was a shortcut to the University of Bolton Stadium. It was the kind of alleyway that encouraged you to walk fast in case you encountered somebody scary coming in the opposite direction. My imagination was playing tricks on me because what would Jenny 'the vixen' Ryan or Peter Kay be doing down there on a Saturday afternoon anyway?

A trip to Bolton these days is a salutary lesson in Football mismanagement and the folly of amateur owners. People with scant knowledge of the game who buy Football Clubs soon learn that being able to afford to buy a football club is God's way of telling you that you have too much money.

In 2005 the Trotters finished sixth in the Premier League, qualifying for the UEFA cup and acquitted themselves well in subsequent seasons until they were relegated to the Championship in 2012. Like many clubs, their ownership had become more complex as their financial problems had intensified. They had started the current season in the Championship after being promoted from League One but the team's performance was dwarfed by a succession of winding up petitions, debts being written off, wages unpaid or late and mystery buyers who subsequently vanish.

Most of these scenarios were familiar to Leeds United fans of course but seeing the purpose built stadium with its integral hotel, the empty seats and general apathy reminded us that we now have an owner who runs a proper business and a club of which we can be proud.

Bolton Wanderers 0 Leeds United 1

15th December 2018

Bolton Wanderers

Alnwick, Taylor, Lowe, Vela, Buckley (Wildschut (72), Noone, Hobbs, Olkowski, Williams (Oztumer 80), Magennis (Doidge 75), Wheater.
Unused Substitutes: Matthews, Donaldson, Wilson, O'Neill.

Leeds

Peacock – Farrell, Shackleton, Jansson, Phillips, Douglas, Forshaw, Klich, Baker (Clarke 45), Alioski, Hernandez (Halme 90), Roofe (Bamford 61).
Unused Substitutes: Huffer, Roberts, Harrison, Davies.

Referee: R Jones

Attendance: 17,484

The gifted but inconsistent Samu Saiz had stated a wish to return to his native Spain a couple of days earlier. United acceded to his wish and he later joined Getafe on loan with an option for them to buy him at the end of the season. He had played his part in the revival particularly earlier in the season but nagging doubts about his attitude and motivation remained in many people's minds. This was compounded when none of the rest of the team wished him well on social media at the time of his departure.

Freezing horizontal rain was never going to assist this game to be a classic and so the first half proved. A more boring, turgid display could not be imagined. Bolton employed the reliable tactic of 'hoofball' and Leeds used a slow build up which was far removed from the quick attacks which had left the rest of the Championship reeling at the start of the season.

In the second half, the ineffectual Baker was replaced by Jack Clarke who put some snap into the proceedings.

Before very long, a tired looking Kemar Roofe was replaced by Patrick Bamford. Very shortly after this, a lovely move culminated in an inch perfect pass from Pablo Hernandez which BAMFORD (66) calmly netted.

United's performance improved from this point on but they were not without a scare or two. The closest was when Bolton keeper Alnwick tried a speculative pitch length shot which woke Peacock – Farrell from his soggy slumbers.

Not a pretty game but another three points in the bag.

Position in Championship Table After Match: 1st.

'With that possession we might have thought we would have created more chances but it wasn't the case. It was a hard win but a deserved one. We had the possession but we didn't have chances to score.'
Marcelo Bielsa

Aston Villa 2 Leeds United 3

Michael Gill

23rd December 2018

Nyland, Chester,Whelan (Bjaarnason 73), McGinn, Bolasie (Hogan 83), Hourihane, Bree, Abraham, Hutton, Kodjia (ElGhazi 62), Elmohamady.
Unused Substitutes: Bunn, Davis, Adomah, Revan.

Leeds United

Peacock – Farrell, Ayling, Jansson, Phillips, Davis (Shackleton 78), Klich, Forshaw, Alioski, Harrison (Clarke 45), Hernandez, Roofe.
Unused Substitutes: Huffer, Baker, Halme, Gotts.

Referee: A Madley

Attendance: 41,411

For once, United played in front of a bigger crowd than at home. At the eleventh hour Barry Douglas had to drop out and Leif Davis made his first start for the Whites. The unfortunate Patrick Bamford had also picked up an injury in training. This setback was unrelated to his previous injury.

Disaster struck after only five minutes when Hourihane passed to McGinn who teed up ABRAHAM (5) to put Villa in front. Harrison almost equalised but scuffed his shot.

United had hardly caught their breath when they found themselves two down. HOURIHANE (17) hit a fine 25 yarder to do the business for Villa.

United stuck to their game plan and continued to chase Villa but they retired at half time without making any inroads into the deficit.

Clarke replaced Harrison at half time as United sought to freshen things up.

It was CLARKE (56) who forced United back into the game. He weaved his way into the box and scored with a nice individual effort.

The Whites now had the bit between their teeth and JANSSON (61) headed home a well taken Pablo
Hernandez corner.

As the game slipped into added on time, it was looking increasingly like a draw, until Leeds broke forward and Alioski crossed the ball which was only cleared as far as ROOFE (90 + 5) who gratefully smashed the ball into the back of the net, causing uproar at the Leeds End.

This was a swashbuckling performance which exemplified the fighting spirit of the team.

Position in Championship Table After Match: 1st.

'We were all just so overwhelmingly happy – maybe too much. We were satisfied with the draw, so we felt euphoric when the ball went in so late on'
Marcelo Bielsa

Leeds United 3 v Blackburn Rovers 2

26th December 2018

Leeds United

Peacock – Farrell, Douglas, Jansson, Phillips, Ayling (Shackleton 69), Forshaw, Klich, Hernandez, Alioski, Clarke (60), Roofe.
Unused Substitutes: Huffer, Baker, Davis, Halme, Gotts.

Blackburn

Raya, Nyambe (Reed 62), Williams, Rodwell (Smallwood 69), Armstrong (Rothwell 75), Graham, Bell, Mulgrew, Dack, Lenihan, Evans.
Unused Substitutes: Leutwiler, Downing, Palmer, Nuttall.

Referee S Martin

Attendance 34,863

Boxing Day saw the visit of Blackburn Rovers. It also saw United riding their luck again.

There was no sign of the drama to come when the Whites took the lead. Jack Harrison had cut the ball back and sent a killer cross in front of the goal. WILLIAMS (33) could only turn the ball into his own net

By the time that the break came around, the Whites had not added to this score and hopes of a routine, comfortable win were in the balance.

The game had scarcely restarted when Ayling brought Mulgrew down in the box. MULGREW (47) picked himself up, dusted himself down and scored from the resultant penalty.

Try as they might, United could not take the initiative. Roofe, Hernandez, Klich Forshaw and Douglas all came close but the Whites still couldn't convert.

Then hearts were broken when Phillips brought Rothwell down and MULGREW (90) found the net from a 30 yard free kick.

Leeds fought on into added on time and were rewarded when ROOFE (90+1) bundled the ball over the line after a goalmouth scramble which involved Jansson and Hernandez. Goal line technology confirmed that the ball had indeed crossed the line.

In the dying seconds, Hernandez sent a superb cross into the Blackburn box and (ROOFE 90+4) headed home seconds before the final whistle was blown, leaving the seasonal crowd in a state of frenzy.

Position in Championship Table After Match: 1st.

'Even if the two wins look alike, the feeling after the game against Aston Villa is different to the feeling we have today. Because today we had he obligation to win and it was not necessarily the case against Aston Villa.'

Marcelo Bielsa.

Leeds United 0 Hull City 2

December 29th 2018

Leeds United

Peacock – Farrell, Ayling, (Shackleton 77), Jansson, Phillips, Douglas (Roberts 64), Klich, Forshaw, Hernandez, Harrison (Clarke 45), Alioski, Roofe.
Unused Substitutes: Huffer, Baker, Davis, Halme.

Hull City

Marshall, De Wijs, Burke, Stewart, Evandro (Toral 45), Grosicki (Lichaj 74), Kane, Keane (Batty 90), Bowen, Henriksen, Kingsley.
Unused Substitutes: Long, Dicko, McKenzie, Martin.

Referee: J Brooks

Attendance 35,754

Having won the last seven matches, United went into this encounter confidently despite the fact that Hull City was now a much tougher prospect than when the sides had met back in October. Nigel Adkins had spread his influence and the Tigers were currently one of the in form teams of the Championship.

It had been rumoured that Leeds had been running the rule over Hull winger Jarrod Bowen and it was BOWEN (25) who gave the Tigers the lead. Grosicki had put the ball into the box but the Whites had failed to clear it and Bowen was on hand to put the ball in the net.

BOWEN (58) doubled his tally after Peacock – Farrell had made a fine save from Grosicki but was only able to parry it away and the sharpshooter latched on to it.

Throughout the game, United had several opportunities to score but didn't take advantage of any of them. It was a combination of poor finishing and the fact that the Hull goalkeeper Marshall chose this match to play the game of his life.

Nothing lasts for ever and the Whites had consolidated their standing by adding 21 points to their tally by winning the last seven games.

Position in Championship Table After Match: 1st.

'The main features of the Championship is the intensity and the similar level between the teams.'
Marcelo Bielsa

CHAPTER 7

January 2019 – Mixed Results and 'Spygate.'

Nottingham Forest 4 v Leeds United 2

January 1st 2019

Nottingham Forest

Pantillimon, Fox, Colback, Murphy (Appiah 90), Carvalho, Cash, Robinson, Lolley (Osborn 65), Yacob, Darikwa, Hefele (Guedioura 5)
Unused Substitutes Steele, Janko, Yates, Sias.

Leeds United

Peacock – Farrell, Ayling, Jansson, Phillips, Douglas (Roberts78), Forshaw, Klich, Hernandez, Harrison (Clarke 45), Alioski, Roofe.
Unused Substitutes: Huffer, Baker, Davis, Shackleton, Halme.

Referee: D England

Attendance: 29,530

United went behind early when Adam Forshaw tried to pass back but didn't put enough power on it. COLBACK (6) nipped in to round Peacock – Farrell for an avoidable first goal.

Soon there was to be controversy as Jack Harrison was chopped down at the edge of the Forest Penalty Box by Jack Robinson. Despite the fact that the Forest man was the last man, the Referee only gave Robinson a yellow card.

The Whites then had an Alioski header cleared off the line before disaster struck. Phillips was very late with his tackle on Guedioura and the Referee unhesitatingly produced a red card, reducing United to ten men.

Jack Clarke replaced Harrison for the second half and it was not long before the youngster made his presence felt. Klich teed the ball up and CLARKE (52) squeezed the ball past Pantillimon.

Five minutes later, Leeds took the lead to the delight of the travelling fans. From a corner, Pablo Hernandez picked the ball up to pass it to Jansson who headed it across the goal for ALIOSKI (64) to smash home on the volley. Amazing scenes followed as Alioski dived into the crowd to pick out Gaetano Beradi who was standing with the away fans.

The euphoria was short lived however COLBACK (69) equalised, when he picked up a goal from a corner.

Three minutes later, the ten men conceded another goal as a result of a corner as MURPHY (72) headed home.

Forest added insult to injury when Murphy beat the offside trap and teed up OSBORN (76) to ensure the points went to Forest.

The Whites have not been in the habit of losing games after having first taken the lead. Unfortunately hanging on was just too much for the ten men. It was a spirited performance nonetheless.

Position in Championship Table After Match: 1st.

'The change in defence, I had in my mind the whole game. It was to put Jamie Shackleton at full back and Ayling at centre back. Adam Forshaw in the middle but we had to make sacrifice of one of the two wingers. One of the two offensive midfielders or our number nine. We couldn't make a change with Clarke and Alioski, Roofe either and Pablo and Klich either. The team was playing well. On the contrary we could have changed the score from a position where we were losing the game to a position where we were winning the game. So when I had the possibility to take a decision, I couldn't take the two playmakers we had and I couldn't take out the two wingers who were creating danger and I couldn't take the number nine either. If I had taken this decision I would have thought at that moment, I would have thought I was destroying something working well. That's why I didn't take the decision. We also had others like Halme and Leif Davis. We also have to take into account one fact, I could have made the change and I would have, from a defensive point of view, would have avoided the reaction of the opponent. I'm just explaining why I didn't make this decision, it doesn't mean that I took the right decision.'
Marcelo Bielsa

Queens Park Rangers 2 Leeds United 1 (FA Cup)

6th January 2019

Queens Park Rangers

Ingram, Furlong, Bidwell, Hall, Freeman, Cousins, Eze (Smith 90), Scowen, Oteh (Chair 83), Osayi – Samuel (Wszolek 86), Kakay.
Unused Substitutes: Lumley, Manning, Baptiste, Smyth.

Leeds United

Peacock – Farrell, Davis (Odour 87), Halme (Pearce 45), (Temenuzhkov 79), Ayling, Shackleton, Forshaw, Baker, Roberts, Clarke, Alioski, Harrison.
Unused Substitutes: Huffer, Diaz, Stevens, Gotts.

Referee: G Eltringham

Attendance: 11,637

Once again, United made an early exit from this once – proud competition. Despite a lively start, with Roberts grazing the woodwork twice, a disjointed side failed to get to grips with fast – moving Rangers.

Predictably enough, the Hoops went ahead with a penalty which was converted by OTEH (25)

United's hopes soared when they were awarded a free kick just two minute later. Baker smashed a shot which Rangers keeper Matt Ingram could not hold. This left HALME (25) with a simple tap in. This was the giant Finn's first senior goal for the Whites.

Halme did not return for the second half and it was clear that Bielsa's strategy was going to be an attacking one. Winning at all costs seemed to be the plan. Further changes were then made, causing United to lose their shape even more.

Bailey Peacock – Farrell made amazing saves but BIDWELL (75) sealed the victory for Rangers, Leaving United to ponder what might have been.

' I think we deserved to lose. We could not find solutions for the set

pieces. We took decisions that were not useful to us and we did not need to make these kinds of decisions.'
Marcelo Bielsa.

On Thursday 10th January, Derbyshire Police were called to the Derby County Training Ground at Morley Road. They detained a man who was later identified as a Leeds United employee. The man was said to be acting suspiciously outside the perimeter fence of the complex. He was said to be observing a private training session conducted by the Midlands Club. Leeds United were due to play County the following day.

The police questioned and searched the man and ascertained that he had not broken any laws. It was reported that he was wearing sports gear, had a change of clothing in his car and had a small pair of pliers or secateurs in his possession. The fevered imagination of some hysterical sensationalists somehow managed to report this as 'combat gear, pliers and bolt – cutters.' If Derbyshire police hadn't confirmed the true facts, the intruder would have probably been accused of carrying an anti tank gun and a surface to air missile!

A representative of Leeds United was reported to have telephoned Derby but the details of this were very sketchy. However the next bombshell was dropped the following evening. The match was being shown on Sky TV and both managers were interviewed before the match as is customary.

Frank Lampard, National Treasure and Derby Manager said; 'On a sportsman's level its bad in my opinion. If we are going to start talking about culturally I did it somewhere else and it was fine, then that doesn't work for me. I don't believe that it is fine on any level. It has disrupted our build up for this game. People will say I'm standing here making excuses before this game. I will speak about this after the game, win, lose or draw.'
Viewers waited with baited breath for Bielsa. Would he deny responsibility? Would he appear at all? Well of course he did appear

and this is what he said:

'It's true there was someone from Leeds United. The person responsible for this incident is me. I am responsible for it. There is some decision that I need to give. It doesn't matter if this is illegal or legal or if it is right or wrong. For me it's enough that Frank Lampard and Derby County felt that it was not the right thing to do and that I didn't behave well.

Yesterday, I talked to Frank Lampard and he told me that I didn't respect the fair play rules. I have a different point of view on it but the important thing is what Frank Lampard and Derby think. I am the only person responsible for it because I didn't ask the club Leeds United permission to do that.

Without trying to find a justification, I have been using this kind of practice since the qualifications for the World Cup with Argentina. This is not illegal, we have been doing it publicly, we talk about it in the press. For some people it is the wrong thing to do but for other people it is not the wrong thing to do.

Leeds United 2 Derby County 0

11th January 2019.

Leeds United

Peacock – Farrell, Ayling, Cooper, Jansson, Alioski, Klich, Forshaw, Hernandez, Harrison (Shackleton 63), Clarke (Davis 79), Roofe. Unused Substitutes: Huffer, Roberts, Stevens, Halme, Gotts.

Derby County

Carson, Wisdom (Nugent 45), Bryson, Tomori, Keogh, Mount, Lawrence, Marriott (Waghorn 72), Evans (Josefzoon 61), Holmes, Lowe. Unused Substitutes: Roos, Bogle, Huddlestone, Malone.

Referee: A Davies

Attendance: 34,668

Leading up to this game, there seemed to be a lot of negativity about amongst the Leeds fans. No Phillips or Douglas, Hernandez doubtful, threadbare bench – unsustainable.

Yet the Whites started the game like an express train, clearly buoyed by the return of Cooper and the last minute availability of Hernandez. In the first minute, referee Andy Wilson awarded a penalty to Leeds after Alioski had been brought down in the box. However, he had to rescind his decision as the linesman had already flagged for offside.

The Whites did not have to wait too long to take the lead. Jack Clarke picked up a ball from a corner and sent a low cross to ROOFE (20) who made no mistake with his shot. The Whites were in total control with standout performances from Forshaw, Alioski, Roofe and Clarke.

Early in the second half, Clarke put in another brilliant cross which Derby keeper Carson could only tip out to Alioski. The Macedonian crossed the ball to HARRISON (47) who had the simple task of tapping it in.

The upbeat tempo continued until the end of the match and justified Bielsa's selections against QPR. The players who were rested in that game looked very sharp in this one. This was United's most complete performance since the early autumn and the score line flattered clueless Derby. It was also very satisfying to see young Jack Clarke being named Sky Man of the Match.

Position in Championship Table After Match: 1st.

'It was a really complete performance. The supporters knew that this was a really important game for us and they supported us like never before. The team behaved in a way that made the supporters like that.'
Marcelo Bielsa.

However, the 'spying' incident would not go away: Lampard was quoted in various publications on the Saturday as saying:

'Cheating is a big word. If you think about details and gaining advantages, great and good managers do that. But this one is over the line. It is not just a toe over the line it is a hop skip and jump over the line. I'd rather not coach than send people under cover on their hands and knees with pliers and bolt cutters and go and look at the opposition because I respect the opposition.'

He went on to say that training had been disrupted. This is hard to swallow as at no time did the Police enter the training ground and we can only assume that he was misinformed about the bolt cutters.

Leeds Chairman Andrea Radrizzani made a formal apology to Derby. He said: 'The Club will work with our Head Coach and his Staff to remind them of the integrity and honesty which are the foundations which Leeds United is built on.'

It was not known at the time whether Bielsa had agreed to this comment, or even knew that it was going to be made.

The EFL Later announced that they would be holding an investigation into the incident.

On Wednesday 16th January, Leeds United announced that they would be holding a press conference late in the afternoon. Rumours were rife and many fans believed that given his volatile reputation, Bielsa had taken enough criticism over the incident and was about to resign.

On the contrary, Marcelo Bielsa gave a seventy minute Power-Point presentation showing the amazing levels of detail that he goes into when analysing the performance of all of his opponents. For the purpose of the presentation, he invited journalists to choose any of Derby County's games and then demonstrated to them the levels of detailed data that his staff had collected.

He also admitted that he had sent staff to observe every single club in the Championship prior to matches being played. The point that he was making was that the so called spying was a tiny part of the overall analysis.

It is well known that all clubs analyze their opponents, often using the same systems to do so but nobody was left in any doubt of the sheer amount of detail that went into Bielsa's analysis.

As always, he presented the information in his humble, respectful and self-deprecating style and could not do other than impress all but the most biased onlookers.

There are lots of arguments that say that he would have been better to leave the matter alone, once Radrizzani had made his public apology but Bielsa would not have been true to himself and personal integrity of a very high standard is all that matters to this remarkable man.

The aftermath of this presentation caused an even bigger furore. Rival clubs called for sanctions against Leeds. These penalties ranged from a bit of a telling off to a huge fine and some of the more creative or self interested chairmen called for a points deduction.

The English Media were at their Xenophobic worst: 'we don't do things like that here' and 'it might be all right in South America.......'

Many coaches and managers who hadn't grasped the depth of his presentation said things like 'This is nothing new, we all do analysis.' These views came from a wide range of coaches from regular 'Wyscout' account holders to those who favour the back of a cigarette packet.

Over in France, Frank LeBoef and Christoph Dugarry described Bielsa as 'autistic' in a French Radio Phone In show.

Bielsa himself felt that a seventy minute presentation was enough to state his case and to his great credit refused to engage in dialogue about the affair again.

Just over a month later, Leeds United were fined £200,000 and given a severe reprimand by the EFL over the incident. Incredibly, several months later, Bielsa admitted that he had paid the fine with his own money. His explanation was that he saw the issue as his own personal responsibility!

A week after the Derby game, I jumped off the train at Stoke on Trent and walked over the bridge which spans the A500 or 'D' road as it is known locally. I was heading for the city centre to get a bite to eat somewhere near where the shuttle buses start for the Bet 365 Stadium.

I found a quaint old pub called 'The Glebe' and looked to see what was on offer. I ordered a pint of Joules Pale and selected a couple of slabs of cheese and some crackers from the deli counter. On taking stock of my surroundings, I felt as if I was in a time warp. The old advertisements and show cards were for Joules Beer and I had noticed that the pub was signed up as a Joules House outside.

I remembered Joules of Stone in Staffordshire from many years ago and my rag patch memory conjured up one of the advertisements in an old Stoke City programme.
'By Joules it's brewed and by Joules it's good!'

This instantly brought back memories of my first visit to Stoke on Trent. Leeds were playing at the ramshackle Victoria Ground and it was the first match of the 1962 – 63 season.

Don Revie had completed his first full season as manager. United had narrowly avoided relegation to the third tier; finishing 19th. They had achieved this unlikely feat by going on a nine game unbeaten run at the end of the season, beating Newcastle 3 – 0 away in the final game.

Apart from the Don's guidance there was another significant contributor to this turn of events. In March 1962, they had signed Bobby Collins from Everton. At five feet four inches he was shorter than Billy Bremner but he was as hard as nails and as well as making a major contribution himself, he became Bremner's mentor.

In the close season, encouraged by these promising developments, the board decided to loosen their purse strings and made a number of signings. Two of these were major ones and they were both strikers. The first was Jim Storrie from Airdrie who made a major contribution in the coming seasons. The other signing was the great John Charles from Juventus.

Leeds had pocketed a then World Record fee when they sold him for £65,000 to Juventus in 1957 and there was enormous excitement around the city when the club signed him back. The club even increased admission prices for the first two home games in an attempt to recoup some of the £50,000 fee

Unfortunately, Charles was not the man that he had been previously. The years of celebrity and good living in Turin meant that 'The Gentle Giant' was somewhat more gigantic than when he had previously played for Leeds.

He showed some lovely touches and scored a total of three goals but the Whites were lucky to unload him to Roma in October 1962 for a fee of £70,000.

Another football great was playing that day: Stanley Matthews had rejoined his hometown club from Blackpool and was seeing out the twilight days of his career with the Potteries outfit. In this game, he failed to impress, having been roughed up a bit by Bobby Collins and Grenville Hair who showed little respect for the 47 year old veteran.

Look at the teams in the picture of the programme and you will find a great question for any pub quiz. 'In which game did Stanley Matthews, John Charles and Billy Bremner all play at the same time?' I guarantee that not many people will know the answer to that one.

Anyway, Leeds won the game 1 – 0. Jim Storrie scored and it was the first of 27 league and cup goals that the likeable Scot netted that season. Leeds finished in fifth position and the rest as they say is history.

Surely though, Joules Brewery had been swallowed up in the carnage that swept the industry in the sixties and seventies?

Well, of course it had been acquired by Bass Charrington who was in turn taken over in the consolidation that continues today as the big brewers resemble a collection of Russian Dolls, each fitting snugly inside a larger one.

It is not uncommon these days for small independent brewers to licence old names and recipes but what makes this story different is that one of the current directors of Joules, Steve Nuttall acquired a brand licence from the giant Molson Coors and resurrected the whole brand, acquired and restored several of their old pubs and proudly brews the beer in Market Drayton. They now have 40 pubs of their own and also supply the free trade.

Armed with this information from the Joules website, and glowing with goodwill and bonhomie, thinking about United's last performance against Derby, I boarded the shuttle bus for the Bet 365 Stadium. What could possibly go wrong?

Stoke City 2 Leeds United 1

January 19th 2019.

Stoke City

Butland, Bauer, Allen, Williams, Etebo, Afobe, Indi, Adam, Shawcross, Clucas, Campbell (McClean 67),
Unused Substitutes: Federici, Ince, Berahino, Crouch, Edwards, Woods.

Leeds United

Peacock – Farrell, Ayling, Cooper, Jansson, Alioski, Forshaw, Klich (Stephens 76) Hernandez, Clarke, Harrison (Roberts 61), Roofe.

Unused Substitutes: Casilla, Davis, Shackleton, Halme, Gotts.

Referee: G Ward

Attendance: 28,586

Nathan Jones was looking for his first win having been appointed just over a week earlier. He had overseen two defeats: One away to Brentford in the Championship and embarrassingly against neighbours Shrewsbury in the FA Cup at home. Jones had experienced phenomenal success at Luton Town but this was a big step up for him.

After their win against Derby, Leeds entered the game with confidence. New goalkeeper, Kiko Casilla from Real Madrid sat this one out on the bench.

Veteran Charlie Adam had the first chance of the game and nearly scored with a volley. Both sides were threatening with Hernandez and Roofe coming close for Leeds. Near the end of the first half, both Cooper and Jansson came close with headers. The game was evenly matched and although United had the lion's share of the possession, the chances were about even.

Early in the second half Cooper and Klich failed to clear headers and CLUKAS (49) volleyed home.

Worse was to come as Jansson was sent off after receiving a second yellow card after a clumsy tussle with Afobe.

Nevertheless, United pushed hard for an equaliser with Roberts coming close and a Luke Ayling header only to be denied by a fantastic save from Butland.

Following a good build up, the strong running play of McClean was rewarded when he struck a fine cross and ALLEN (88) stuck the ball home at the back post.

ALIOSKI (90 + 5) netted a consolation goal for the Whites but there was hardly time to restart the match.

Michael Gill

Position in Championship Table After Match: 1st.

'We can't say that we ignored the features of the opponent. We just didn't take advantage of the possibilities we had. We had all the resources that we needed to win this game, but we did not play well enough.'
Marcelo Bielsa

The next trip was up to Rotherham and because of the continuing Northern Rail strike, I travelled with my old friends, The Thames Valley Whites. They are ably run by Steve Griffin and mainly cover Oxfordshire, Berkshire and Buckinghamshire. They picked me up at Northampton Services and we had a very pleasant stop for a couple of pints of Pedigree on the way.

Now for some reason, I had it in my mind that Northampton Services were situated Northbound only. My reason for this mistake was that you have to leave the motorway at junction 15a to access them.

It was only after they dropped me off on the way back that I realised that there were services on both sides of the motorway and that I found myself on the Southbound Services while my car was safely parked on the other side of the M1!

To my relief, I noticed that there was a connecting covered footbridge. My joy was short lived however when I realised that it was locked and in darkness. No matter, I found a member of the cleaning staff and explained my predicament. The man was very helpful but his English was not that good. Eventually, after shaking his head a couple of times, he wrote a code for me on a piece of paper and retreated into the warmth of the café.

I tapped the code into the keypad and opened the door to the footbridge. After climbing the steps gingerly as the only light in there was from the headlights of the vehicles below, I sniffed the damp, putrid air and made my way across the footbridge, realising that my phone was dead. The scene was like something out of a low budget horror movie and I tried to put away the thought that was forming in my mind that maybe the door at the other end would be locked also. The door was locked but only from the outside and so I was able to slip the bolt and make my way to my car, almost as thankful for my escape as I was for the three points which Leeds had picked up earlier in the afternoon!

Rotherham 1 v Leeds 2

26th January 2019.

Rotherham

Rodak, Mattock, Vaulks, Ajayi, Forde, Taylor (Yates 75), Towell (Crooks 85), Robertson, Smith (Vassell 82), Ragett, Jones.
Unused Substitutes: Price, Vyner, Wood, Palmer.

Leeds United

Casilla, Ayling, Cooper, Phillips, Alioski, Forshaw, Klich, Hernandez (Davis 90 + 6), Harrison (Shackleton 88), Roofe, Clarke (Roberts 45).
Unused Substitutes: Peacock – Farrell, Pearce, Halme.

Referee: T Robinson

Attendance: 11,259

'Twenty yards or thirty yards everywhere we go
Forty yards or fifty yards, Klich is scoring goals.'

This song was originally sung in the Autumn when the Polish International was scoring eye catching goals. It seemed that as soon as the song caught on, the goals dried up. The brace of goals he scored in this match were not thirty yards or indeed twenty yards but they were most welcome nonetheless!

After a torrid first half with few chances for either side apart from a well taken goal from AJAYI (27), the Whites stumbled off the pitch. I even heard a few boos from some of our less forgiving brethren.

Jack Clarke who had been having a tough time was replaced by Tyler Roberts who looked lively.

United mounted wave after wave of attack and soon they were rewarded. KLICH (51) netted the equaliser via an elbow and backside as the ball tic tac toed its way into the net.

The Whites kept the pressure up and were rewarded with a second goal. KLICH (86) netted the winner with four minutes of normal time to go. Jack Harrison had crossed the ball with unerring accuracy.

This was a tough game but a satisfying one for despite their lowly position, Rotherham had a good home record.

Kiko Casilla looked sharp and his distribution was fast and accurate.

At the end Bielsa gave a rare show of emotion as he hugged colleague Pablo Quiroga.

Position in Championship Table After Match: 1st

'In the first half, the team had the ball but we didn't create many chances and in the second half we had the ball but created chances.' Marcelo Bielsa

CHAPTER 8

*February – Revenge for Norwich
and a shock at Shepherds Bush.*

Leeds United 1 v Norwich City 3

February 2nd 2019.

Leeds United

Casilla, Ayling, Jansson, Cooper, Alioski, Forshaw, Klich, Roberts (Bamford 63), Harrison (Douglas 45), Hernandez (Clarke 45), Roofe.
Unused Substitutes: Peacock – Farrell, Phillips, Shackleton, Gotts.

Norwich City

Krul, Godfrey, Zimmerman, Vrancic, Lewis, Buendia (McClean 85), Stiepermann, Trybull (Tetty 84), Pukki (Rhodes (87), Hernandez, Aarons.
Unused Substitutes: McGovern, Hanley, Srbeny, Cantwell.

Referee: S Attwell

Attendance: 36,524

The Whites were outclassed by a better team on the day. That's exactly what happened. No beating about the bush. Was there poor refereeing? Yes. Disallowed goal and penalty claims? Yes. Nevertheless, the undeniable truth is that United were as poor and Norwich were as good as in the reverse fixture last August.

The early concession of a goal put the Whites on the back foot. VRANCIC (5) scored from a free kick after sloppy defending from Pontus Jansson.

Forshaw was then caught in possession to give Vrancic another chance. His shot was blocked but the prolific PUKKI (35) was on hand to slide the ball home from close quarters.

In the second half VRANCIC (75) all but wrapped it up for the Canaries. United had replaced the uncharacteristically off key Hernandez and Harrison with Clarke and Douglas but the changes failed to make an impact.

Patrick Bamford came on for Tyler Roberts who was arguably United's best performer.

BAMFORD (90 + 5) headed home a 'centre forward's goal' from a corner but it was all too late by then.

The Whites had now lost five of their last seven games.

Position in Championship Table After Match: 2nd.

'We couldn't take our positive moments in the first half hour. We made mistakes in front of our box and helped Norwich to make chances. After they scored, it was hard for us to recover the ball. The way Norwich used the ball in the second half made it difficult for us. It was hard to play deep and attack constantly. This is an indication that the team is not doing very well right now.'
Marcelo Bielsa'

Middlesbrough 1 v Leeds United 1

9th February 2019.

Middlesbrough

Randolph, Shotton, Ayala, Flint, Fry, Friend, Mikel, Howson, Wing (Besic 64), Saville (Clayton 78), Hugill (Assombalonga 77).
Unused Substitutes: Dimi, Downing, Van La Parra, Fletcher.

Leeds United

Casilla, Ayling (Shackleton 80), Jansson, Cooper, Alioski, Phillips, Klich (Roberts 58), Roofe, Harrison, Clarke (Hernandez 45), Bamford.
Unused Substitutes: Peacock – Farrell, Brown, Davis, Halme.

Referee: D England

Attendance: 30,881

The Riverside Stadium had not been a happy hunting ground for United in recent years and they were facing a side which was built in the image and likeness of their manager; Tony Pulis. They were uncompromising, pragmatic, risk averse and often not very pretty to watch. To add to their motivation to win this game, they had just been dumped out of the FA Cup by fourth tier side

Newport County. Coincidentally, this was a fate which had befallen United in the previous season.

As expected, the game was very tightly contested if not a pleasing spectacle to witness. Arguably, the best chance of the first half fell to former Boro striker Patrick Bamford who could only fire wide after a clever lay off from Jack Harrison.

Pablo Hernandez was introduced at the beginning of the second half and injected some much – needed creativity into the attack. He had replaced Clarke who was having a quiet game.

The home side took the lead shortly after the restart as WING (47) was given too much space in the penalty area and neatly slotted in to give Boro the lead.

The game was later halted for twelve minutes. Jack Clarke, who was sat on the bench started feeling unwell and was given oxygen before being taken to hospital. Thankfully this turned out to be no more than a virus but as a precaution, the young star was missing for several games as tests took place to ensure his fitness.

The Whites threw everything at the opposition and were rewarded well into added on time when PHILLIPS (90 + 11) broke Middlesbrough hearts with a late equaliser.

It was a draw that felt like a win and just what United needed to blow any negatives away after the Norwich game.

Position in Championship Table After Match: 1st.

'If we take into account the fifteen minutes of the first half where we were not at ease but apart from this segment I think we dominated the game, we created chances and deserved to score this goal and probably deserved to score other goals.'
Marcelo Bielsa

Leeds United 2 v Swansea City 1

February 13th 2019.

Leeds United

Casilla, Ayling, Cooper, Jansson, Alioski, Phillips, Klich (Shackleton 77), Roofe, Hernandez (Davis 90 +1), Bamford (Roberts 71), Harrison.
Unused Substitutes:Peacock – Farrell, Shackleton, Stevens, Halme.

United made an aggressive start, encouraged by their battling draw at Middlesbrough.

From a corner, Bamford just missed the ball but Alioski picked it up and smashed a shot towards goal. Swansea couldn't hold it and JANSSON (20) found the bottom corner and launched himself into an exuberant celebration.

The Whites continued to dominate the play and Kemar Roofe came close after good work from Matteus Klich.

Later, Alioski sent a superb cross in and it just took the lightest of glancing headers from HARRISON (30) to put United in the driving seat.

Bamford almost joined the fun just before half time but couldn't get his header past Mulder.

In the second half, Mulder was playing out of his skin, denying good efforts from Cooper, Hernandez and Roofe as The Whites failed to see any more rewards for their dominance.

As the clock ran down, Asoro managed to draw a foul in the penalty box and MCBURNIE (87) despatched the resultant spot kick.

Including added on time there was twelve minutes left to play but Leeds held their nerve to hang on to the three points.

Position in Championship Table After Match: 1st.

'It's hard to understand that we only won by one goal of difference because we dominated the game. Because we had many chances to score.

Also we had many actions that could have become chances to score and they didn't become chances to score.'
Marcelo Bielsa

Leeds United 2 v Bolton Wanderers 1

23rd February 2019.

Leeds United

Casilla, Ayling (Shackleton (90 + 4), Cooper, Jansson, Alioski, Phillips, Klich, Roberts (Dallas 81), Hernandez, Bamford, Harrison.
Unused Substitutes: Peacock – Farrell, Brown, Davis, Stevens, Gotts.

Bolton Wanderers

Matthews, Lowe, Beevers, Wheater, Donaldson (Ameobi 74), Noone (Buckley 82), Olkowski, Connolly, O'Neill, Williams (Murphy 86), Magennis.
Unused Substitutes: Williams, Little, Vela, Hobbs.

Referee: T Harrington

Attendance: 34,144

Once again, United faced lowly Bolton. Sadly there was no sign of the Lancashire Club's financial difficulties improving. Players' wages were being paid late and it was a credit to the team that they were winning any games at all.

Although they made hard work of it, the Whites came home with all three points. Familiar statistics confirmed their superiority but in the end a single goal margin had to suffice.

A rare penalty was awarded after good work from Tyler Roberts. BAMFORD (16) dispatched it confidently. The expected rout did not materialise and Bolton levelled the scores when BEEVERS (23) drove the ball home after a goal line clearance from Jack Harrison.

In the second half, United seized the initiative with a bizarre goal.

As we were lamenting the poor quality of his cross, the ball eluded Remi Matthews in the Bolton goal and curled into the top corner. ALIOSKI (68) found himself on the score sheet and odd though the goal was, it was a vital one.

United carried on storming the Bolton goal but they could not breach the Trotters defence.

The customary nervous finish ensued and when the final whistle was blown there was a huge cheer of relief.

Position in Championship Table After Match: 3rd.

'It's a game very similar to other games we have played so far. We had chances to score and we didn't score goals and we suffered on set pieces. I think this was the axis of the game. It was a team who fought a lot. We had many chances to score and missed many goals and the dangerous actions created by the opponent were on set pieces especially.'
Marcelo Bielsa

My old friend Mike and myself called into a pub in Ladbroke Grove called the Elgin en route to Loftus Road for the Queens Park Rangers game. After rejecting two pints of a sour, cloudy concoction which was long past its glory, we played safe with a Craft Beer and switched to Camden Pale which was fine. It was like turning the clock back fifty years in London, having to drink keg beer to ensure a decent pint. We then repaired to the Fez Mangal for the best and cheapest Turkish Grill that I have ever tasted.

We were seated amongst the QPR fans on Ellerslie Road but as the game progressed, there was no danger of my identifying myself as a Leeds fan by getting over excited!

Queens Park Rangers 1 Leeds United 0

26th February 2019.

Queens Park Rangers

Lumley, Furlong, Bidwell, Hall, Freeman (Scowen 86), Cousins, Eze (Osayi – Samuel (77), Luongo,Wszolek, Wells (Hemed (83), Leistner.
Unused Substitutes: Ingram, Manning, Smith, Lynch.

Leeds United

Casilla, Ayling (Dallas 73), Cooper, Jansson, Alioski (Brown 81), Phillips (Douglas 65), Klich, Harrison, Bamford, Hernandez.
Unused Substitutes: Peacock – Farrell, Beradi, Shackleton, Gotts.

Referee: A Davies

Attendance: 14,763

QPR had lost the previous seven games but for some reason I was not feeling too confident. The Hoops were enjoying an extended run in the FA Cup and this was a rearranged game which was effectively the game in hand. Winning would mean returning to the top of the table and was the outcome which was widely expected.

United started well and Pablo Hernandez fired just wide after a good build up by Tyler Roberts and Patrick Bamford.

The Whites then had a strong claim for a penalty when a Bamford strike appeared to be blocked by the lower arms of Leistner. Phillips also had two chances and United appeared to be bossing the game.

Liam Cooper received a head injury and was missing for the closing stages of the first half as he received treatment and was assessed.

The game had barely restarted for the second half when Massimo Luongo burst down the right wing
and sent a low cross to FREEMAN (49) who slotted the ball home.

Alioski almost repeated his eccentric effort against Bolton when he nearly scored directly from a corner but Lumley managed to tip it over the bar. Later Barry Douglas missed an absolute sitter when Hernandez sent a superb pass to him in the box.

It was all Leeds but somehow the Hoops managed to hold out and keeper Lumley was having the game of his life as he dealt with shot after shot from the rampant Whites.

Somehow, Rangers had managed to record their first Championship victory of the year and United's game in hand was a game in hand no more.

The following day a photograph of Bielsa appeared in the press. He was squatting in the tunnel, alone and with his head in his hands. It was the absolute picture of dejection, despair and loneliness. He is a man who rarely shows his emotions and so just like the shot of the triumphal hug against Rotherham, this photograph endeared him to the Leeds fans. Here was a man who cared as much as we did and experienced the same highs and lows that we experience every week.

Position in Championship Table After Match: 3rd.

'We didn't take advantage of the first half. In our best moment of the first half we had Liam Cooper out so we couldn't dominate as we had been doing. In the first half apart from the first minutes, our team started to dominate the game and create danger until the last ten minutes where Liam Cooper was absent we couldn't keep dominating.'
Marcelo Bielsa

CHAPTER 9

*March 2019 Four Great Wins and
an Undeserved Setback.*

Leeds United 4 West Bromwich Albion 0

March 1st 2019.

Leeds United

Casilla, Ayling, Cooper, Jansson, Alioski, Phillips, Klich, Hernandez, Roberts (Shackleton (90 + 2), Bamford, Harrison (Dallas 77).
Unused Substitutes: Peacock – Farrell, Douglas, Beradi, Brown, Gotts.

West Bromwich Albion

Johnstone, Adarabioyo, Hegazi, Dawson, Holgate, Barry (Morrison 63), Livermore, Harper (Field 65), Robson – Kanu (Montero 70), Rodriguez, Gayle.
Unused Substitutes: Bond, Bartley, Townsend, Murphy.

Referee: T Robinson

Attendance: 35,808

Three days after the Queens Park Rangers game, United were in action again. After all the navel – gazing and analysis that followed the failed encounter with the Hoops, the Whites came back in style as they have done so often following a below par performance.

Despite playing their third game in only six days, Leeds tore Albion apart with one of their best displays of the season.

While latecomers were still taking their seats HERNANDEZ (1) spotted a gap in the defence and whizzed a fine shot into the top corner.

What happened next was truly amazing.

Clinical finishing from Bamford, Silky skills and great assists from Roberts, great defending from Phillips, Cooper and Jansson. As for Alioski, he kept popping up all over the pitch in a performance that gave a new meaning to box to box play.

BAMFORD (28) added a second after some deft footwork from Tyler Roberts At half time, the players left the field to a deafening and deserved ovation.

In the second half the unstoppable Roberts once again found BAMFORD (63) who hit a deflected shot pas the hapless Johnstone.

In the dying minutes of the game, the energetic ALIOSKI (90+ 2) reaped the rewards for his non stop power play performance. Jamie Shackleton had broken into the box and left the Macedonian a simple task of tapping the ball into the net. This prompted Alioski to orchestrate one of his weird celebrations, surrounded by his ecstatic team mates.

Above all this was a team effort and an indication of how far Marcelo Bielsa has taken the team in such a small period of time.

Position in Championship Table After Match: 1st.

'Tuesday (QPR game) *I shouldn't have shown myself so disappointed. I should be very happy tonight. There's a group is around the players that deserves some credit because it is the third game in a week. We have to give some credit to the fitness department and Medical Department because they have an important role in making the players such a great physical performance such as tonight. This group helped the players even if I insist on the fact that the effort came from the heart of each player.'*
Marcelo Bielsa

Bristol City 0 v Leeds United 1

March 9th 2019.

Bristol City

O'Leary, DaSilva, Webster, Wright, Callas, Pack (Palmer 79), Brownhill, O'Dowda (Weimann 59), Semenyo (Taylor 58), Patterson, Diedhiou.
Unused Substitutes: Marinovic, Kelly, Eliassson, Hunt.

Leeds United

Casilla, Alioski, Cooper, Jansson, Ayling, Phillips, Klich (Beradi

83), Roberts, Harrison (Douglas 75), Hernandez, Bamford (Dallas 57).
Unused Substitutes: Peacock – Farrell, Brown, Shackleton, Gotts.

Referee: P Bankes.

Attendance: 24,832

The Atyeo Stand at Ashton Gate is behind one of the goals and could house 4,200 fans. The Whites were only allocated 2,600 despite the fact that this area is completely segregated from the rest of the ground. The front ten or so rows were covered over. The reason given was the all inclusive excuse of 'police advice.' A number of Leeds fans were frustrated with this situation and had purchased tickets in the other parts of the ground. As a reward for their initiative, their names were checked against the Leeds database and their tickets cancelled. Glad you can afford to throw away about £45,000. Not good business City!

United started like a house on fire and battered the Bristol goal right from the kick off. Ayling headed across the goal and BAM-FORD (9) slid the ball in at the far post. In doing this, he managed to wrap himself around the post and play was held up for a while as the striker received attention. After this, he never looked quite the same and was eventually withdrawn after 57 minutes.

Luke Ayling was having a great game and seemed to be revelling in the catcalls of his former admirers. Despite their reduced numbers, the Leeds support was in good voice and their continuing wall of noise helped to bring the three points home.

It shouldn't have been such a close thing because The Robins did not have too many ideas in front of goal. On the few occasions that they did pose a threat, Jansson, Cooper and Phillips were on hand to snuff it out. Casillo also kept sharp when he was needed.

The last thirty minutes seemed to drag as United seemed content to sit back and let City back into the game Nevertheless, this was a hard earned and precious three points.

Position in Championship Table After Match: 2nd.

'I came to be part of a programme that has goals and we know what are the goals of the team, of the city, of the fans and of the players.'
Marcelo Bielsa

Reading 0 Leeds United 3

12th March 2019.

Reading

Martinez, Yiadom, Moore, Swift, Baker, Barrow (Olise 69), Miazga, Meite, Blackett, East (Harriott 53). Loader (McCleary 81).

Leeds United

Casilla, Ayling (Dallas 56), Cooper, Jansson, Alioski, Phillips, Klich (Douglas 75), Harrison, Roberts (Shackleton 69), Bamford, Hernandez.
Unused Substitutes: Peacock – Farrell, Beradi, Brown, Gotts.

Referee: G Ward

Attendance: 17,101

Reading almost opened the scoring when former Leeds under achiever, Modou Barrow was closed down quickly by Kiko Casilla.

Three minutes later, Ayling crossed from the right, Bamford did a cheeky step over to leave KLICH (14) with the simple task of side footing it into the net.

HERNANDEZ (22) added a second, turning quickly in the box to fire home off the far post, sending the visiting fans wild.

The game was practically sewn up when Bamford played the ball to HERNANDEZ (43). The little Spaniard smashed a fine 25 yarder into the top corner.

United didn't add to their tally in the second half with profligate finishing from Bamford, Hernandez, Roberts and Harrison.

Nevertheless it was a comprehensive win and meant that United had won the last three games, scoring eight goals without reply.

Position in Championship Table After Match: 1st.

'If you have a look at the table, you can only reach the conclusion that we have many games to play. Taking this into account, we will have to win every game. At least we will try to win every game. It was a fair result and we could have scored more goals but we could also have conceded a goal.'
Marcelo Bielsa

Leeds United 0 v Sheffield United 1

16th. March 2019.

Leeds United

Casilla, Ayling (Dallas 77), Cooper, Jansson, Alioski, Phillips, Klich (Clarke 77), Roberts, Hernandez, Bamford, Harrison, (Douglas 57). Unused Substitutes: Peacock – Farrell, Beradi, Shackleton, Gotts.

Sheffield United

Henderson, Baldock, Stevens, Cranie, Fleck, O'Connor, Basham, (Lundstram 90), Egan, Norwood, Sharp, McGoldrick (Dowell 88). Unused Substitutes: Hogan, Coutts, Stearman, Duffy, Moore.

Referee: D Coote

Attendance: 37,004

This was billed as the 'must win' big one and the match of the season. Whoever won the game would be second in the table by the end of it.

Sadly, yet another dominant display by The Whites was to end in disappointment. Sheffield United stole all three points at Elland Road.

Billy Sharp had given Liam Cooper the slip and BASHAM (71) scored totally against the run of play.

The Whites had 70% of the possession but could not put the ball in the net. The Blades goal was put under siege after multiple chances went begging, especially in the first half.

The game at Bramall Lane earlier in the season had been much tighter and yet United had managed to nick it. This time around Bamford and Roberts could have had two goals each had they taken their chances.

Pontus Jansson took a heavy knock and had to play in attack as all the substitutes had been used.

Close to the end, Kiko Casilla was sent off after bringing Sharp down. Pontus Jansson had to take the gloves for the same reason as he had been a makeshift forward.

Eight games left and still everything to play for as the Championship 'musical chairs' game entered another phase.

Position in Championship Table After Match: 2nd.

'Nobody can say this is a crucial result because there are still 24 points at stake. I don't want to underestimate their victory but if you analyse the game, we can't be unsatisfied even if we can be disappointed with the result. We created a lot of chances against a very good side.'
Marcelo Bielsa

Leeds United 3 Millwall 2

30th March 2019.

Leeds United

Peacock – Farrell, Ayling, Cooper, Jansson (Clarke 67), Alioski (Douglas 45), Phillips, Klich (Forshaw 75), Roberts, Harrison, Hernandez, Bamford.

Millwall

Martin, Meredith (O'Brien 84), Cooper, Wallace, Thompson (Elliott 87), Gregory, Romeo, Pearce, Tunnicliffe (Morison 86), Leonard, Marshall.
Unused Substitutes: McLaughlin, Hutchinson, Williams, Archer.

Referee: D Bond

Attendance: 34,910

Earlier in the week, former Leeds striker Steve Morison had tried
to up the ante in the press. Why he decided to drag up 'Spygate'
only he knows but clearly it didn't have any adverse effect on the
Whites.

Leeds came back from behind twice and had the luxury of a
missed penalty in a nerve – jangling clash at Elland Road.

The home fans hearts sank as Marshall put the Lions ahead after
only ten minutes. A few minutes later, Patrick Bamford squan-
dered the chance to equalise by sending a weak penalty at David
Martin after Alioski had been felled in the box.

The ever reliable HERNANDEZ (34) was there to level the scores
after Ayling pulled the ball back from the by line.

Millwall took the lead again early in the second half after a desperate lunge by Liam Cooper after he was left exposed when Barry
Douglas had been caught in possession near the half way line.
MARSHALL (56) picked himself up, dusted himself down and buried the resultant penalty.

As the minutes started to tick away, United stuck to their game
plan and were rewarded when Barry Douglas redeemed himself
by sending in a fine cross. AYLING (71) headed the ball out of Martin's reach and into the net.

Twelve minutes later, Tyler Roberts showed some lovely skill on
the ball as he was able to pull the ball back and place it in the path

of the grateful HERNANDEZ (83) who smashed it into the net to the delight of the Elland Road crowd.

It was even sweeter when we learned that Sheffield United had lost their game to Bristol City.

Position in Championship Table After Match: 2nd.

'I can still feel my heart! Every game we play, we just have to play the game. Don't be thinking about any possibility of the results of other teams.'
Marcelo Bielsa

CHAPTER 10

April & May 2019

I never visit Birmingham without calling into The Birmingham Irish Centre on Deritend High Street. This institution is a veritable oasis in a very edgy area. It's also about half way between New Street Station and St. Andrews.

Having arrived in good time, I ordered their all day breakfast, washed down with a couple of pints of very inexpensive Guinness and then proceeded to torture myself by watching Norwich v Queens Park Rangers on their TV screen.

Having lost interest in this when Norwich went four goals up, I went into 'Minstrel Music' which is owned and run by John Fitzgerald. John's shop has been part of The Birmingham Irish Centre for thirty five years and sells all sorts of Irish goodies, not just things associated with music.

In his younger days, John was Lead singer with The Castaways Showband who toured the Irish Dance halls in the UK from Cricklewood to Glasgow. I had a good chat with John about the old days because of course he knows Leeds very well having played the former Shamrock Club and other venues which have long since closed.

I left, wishing him well and saying that I hoped that I would not see him next year because Leeds would be in the Premier League. Gary Monk had other ideas!

Birmingham City 1 v Leeds United 0

6th April 2019.

Birmingham City

Camp, Colin, Dean, Morrison, Pederson, Mahoney (Jota 76), Gardner (Davis 45), Kieftenbeld (Harding 57), Maghoma, Adams, Jutkiewicz.
Unused Substitutes: Roberts, Vassell, Mrabti, Trueman.

Leeds United

Casilla, Jansson, Phillips, Cooper, Ayling, Klich (Clarke 70) Alioski, Hernandez, Roberts, Harrison (Dallas 45), Bamford (Roofe 70).
Unused Substitutes: Peacock – Farrell, Beradi, Forshaw, Shackleton.

Referee: M Dean

Attendance: 24,197

Once again, United were left to regret a bag full of mixed chances as Birmingham edged to a narrow victory.

The first real opportunity fell to Patrick Bamford, who smashed Luke Ayling's lovely cross against the post. Very shortly afterwards, Lucas Jutkiewicz stepped over the ball to allow ADAMS (29) to stick the ball into the corner of the Leeds net.

In the second half, Stuart Dallas came on for Jack Harrison. Patrick Bamford missed another chance when he shot the Irishman's cross over the bar. It was just not Bamford's day as he forced a fingertip save from Lee Camp with his next effort.

United then introduced Roofe and Clarke for Bamford and Klich but could not break the Blues defence down. In fact there was plenty of action at the other end. Kiko Casilla kept the Whites in the game with a series of fine reaction saves.

Birmingham are now the only club to do the double over Leeds. The fans' nerves were not improved by news that Sheffield United had held on to their lead over Preston to move into second place, just one point ahead of United. The vagaries of the fixture system had Leeds visiting Preston in midweek, while the Blades were due to play Birmingham. Cool heads will be needed.

Position in Championship Table After Match: 3rd.

'The position of Klich did not help the team to create chances in attack. After they scored, we moved his position and he started to attack more. Our attacking improved. The decisions I made from the bench couldn't change the result in the way I wanted to. The changes I made weren't enough so I would criticise myself for that. In the last twenty minutes, we couldn't create chances. We had a lot of options on the bench to make changes and the decisions on the changes were not the best ones.

Michael Gill

I take responsibility about the positioning of Klich too.'
Marcelo Bielsa

Preston North End 0 Leeds United 2

April 9th 2019.

Preston North End

Rudd, Fisher, Earl, Pearson, Storey, Davies, Nmecha (Stockley 87), Johnson, Maguire (Ledson 70), Browne, Robinson (Moult 58). Unused Substitutes: Crowe, Rafferty, Ginnelly, Huntington.

Leeds United

Casilla, Ayling, Cooper, Bamford (Roofe 90), Alioski, Roberts (Forshaw 83), Jansson, Hernandez, Harrison (Beradi 77), Phillips, Klich.
Unused Substitutes: Peacock – Farrell, Dallas, Shackleton, Stevens.

Referee: R. Jones

Attendance: 18,109

As expected, Marcelo Bielsa kept faith in the team that had failed at Birmingham. Bamford was again preferred to Roofe and to everybody's relief, Pablo Hernandez was ruled fit to start.

The Leeds fans were treated to a different Patrick Bamford. This was not the languid stroller but rather a hard to handle hustler who used his weight and height as well as his considerable skill. This improved version of the striker was almost as much fun to watch as the two fine goals which he scored.

The game was evenly balanced in the first half although United had the lion's share of the chances. Bamford, Klich both came close before half time.

In the second half, it was Bamford's hustling and harrying that led to the incident which changed the game. Bamford had latched on to a nice through ball and was about to give Pearson the slip when the accident – prone defender brought him to the ground. Although Pearson had already picked up a yellow card, he was handed a red one as he was adjudged to be the last line of defence. This was his third red card of the season and he left the field to the voices of the Leeds fans reminding him that it was time to go and wishing him 'bon voyage.'

Phillips curled the resultant free kick over the bar but it was not long before the Whites scored. BAMFORD (62) took a throw in and on the return, wriggled himself free before letting fly with a twenty yard screamer which found the top left hand corner of Rudd's goal.

BAMFORD (76) added a second, heading home a finely weighted cross from Matteus Klich. This effectively ended the contest and once again, United had stormed back fighting after being defeated in the previous game as they nudged their way back to second place.

Position in Championship Table After Match: 2nd.

'The first half was the best moment to make an evaluation of the team. It was a very difficult game but we could impose in the first half. We played against a team who I like how they play, I like their style, their coach and the players they have. We overcame the opponent with a lot of effort in the first half when the physical tempo of the game was very high.
In the second half after the red card we solved this game more easily, until the last minute, they created one ball in the channel then they created the chance.
I am proud of the team because all the players played at a high level of performance.'
Marcelo Bielsa

On the day of the Sheffield Wednesday match, I left the White Hart early as I was meeting someone in the Centenary Pavilion. The Sheffield United v Millwall game was reaching its final stages and at 1 – 0 to the Blades it was looking like a win for us today would just keep us the single point ahead of them and that any other result would see us slip into third place.

Then a penalty was awarded to Millwall and both agony and ecstasy were experienced as John Egan made a fine one handed save for Sheffield United and was sent off for his trouble. Marshall then smashed the spot kick against the crossbar to the gasps and groans of the assembled multitude.

That looked like that until Millwall defender Cooper equalised with a diving header. There was stunned silence in the pavilion, followed by pandemonium! Plastic beer cups were thrown in the air and chaos ensued. If that wasn't a sufficient incentive for the Whites to win, nothing else would be.

Leeds United 1 v Sheffield Wednesday 0

13th April 2019

Leeds United

Casilla, Jansson, Phillips, Beradi, Ayling, Klich (Forshaw 77), Roberts, Alioski, Hernandez, Bamford (Roofe 64), Harrison (Dallas 86).
Unused Substitutes: Peacock – Farrell, Davis, Shackleton, Clarke.

Sheffield Wednesday

Westwood, Palmer, Lees, Hector, Fox, Reach (Marco Matias 41), Hutchinson, Bannan, Boyd, Fletcher (Nuhiu 76), Hooper (Forestieri 66).

Referee: T Robinson

Attendance: 36,461

United suffered an early setback when Liam Cooper had to withdraw from the match after pulling a muscle in the warm up.

However, this was a magnificent performance from Bielsa's men. Mature and polished yet gutsy, Leeds took the initiative to crush a brave Wednesday side.

This was despite the fact that Wednesday's keeper Kieran Westwood had the game of his life and looked as though he was going to prevent justice being done. He defied goal bound efforts Bamford, Roberts, Harrison and Hernandez, as United held the Wednesday goal under siege.

The breakthrough finally came when Pablo Hernandez hit a sublime pass to HARRISON (65) who coolly slotted the ball into the left hand corner of the net.

Even though nearly half an hour of play remained, United never looked like losing their lead and Alioski even had time for a bit of play acting when he wiped free kick foam on the official's sock without being disciplined!

Position in Championship Table After Match: 2nd.

'It is not a big difference, we have to stay focussed. We needed to create a lot of chances to score the goal. Our objective now is to improve the level of efficiency, as that is important to win the games. When you are winning with only one goal difference, you have to be focussed until the end.'
Marcelo Bielsa

Leeds United 1 v Wigan Athletic 2

19th April 2019.

Leeds United

Casilla, Ayling, Jansson, Beradi, Alioski, Phillips (Forshaw 45), Hernandez, Roberts (Roofe 45), Klich (Jack Clarke 70), Harrison, Bamford.
Unused Substitutes: Peacock – Farrell, Shackleton, Dallas, Davis.

Wigan Athletic

Walton, Byrne, Dunkley, Kipre, Robinson, James (Garner 90+2), Morsy, Massey (Powell 75), Evans, Naismith, Leon Clarke (Olsson 67)
Unused Substitutes: Evans, Roberts, Windass, Gibson.

Referee: S Duncan

Attendance: 34,758

As expected, Nottingham Forest didn't do Leeds any favours as they lost to Sheffield United in the lunch time fixture. The 'what if?' philosophers all put their calculators away and contented themselves with the thought that Leeds would still be three points ahead when they beat Wigan.

The older hands amongst us never had much time for the 'what if?' crowd anyway. It brought to mind the words of Howard Wilkinson who once said that if his Auntie possessed a certain part of the male anatomy then she would have been his uncle!

Not one of the 'iffers' predicted a Wigan win but that's what happened and the automatic promotion pendulum swung again leaving the Whites in third place.

It had started well enough, with Bamford hitting a beauty which Kipre used his hand to clear. He was promptly sent off and the Referee pointed to the spot. Pablo Hernandez hit the ball against the right hand post. It was not a well taken penalty and made us wish that Roofe had started. Not to worry because BAMFORD (17) brought the ball under control and smashed in a beautiful shot. All the faithful then sat back and looked forward to the prospect of United improving their goal difference against ten men.

Instead, The Whites threw it away with MASSEY (44) scoring the equaliser to close the first half.

MASSEY (62) added another and it just didn't seem like United's day. They battered and bashed the Wigan defence but all to no avail and left us praying for one of the famous bounce backs against Brentford on Easter Monday.

'Everything was in our favour. Destiny gave us a hand – a red card for the opponent, a penalty we missed – fifteen chances to score. There's no doubt that I bear the responsibility for this moment. I'm very sad but I'm very motivated.'
Marcelo Bielsa

Position in Championship after the Match: 3rd.

Griffin Park Brentford should be one of my favourite football stadiums. With a pub at each corner of the ground, it is surrounded by tight terraces of houses. Many of the homeowners have stalls in front of their houses on match days selling hot dogs, burgers and other goodies. It is also in the heartland of Fullers Brewery and arguably the best Curries in Britain can be had just up the road at Southall.

Yet I can't warm to it. This is probably because Leeds have not won there since 1950 Unfortunately, I was not at that match owing to the oppressive and unfair decision of my parents who would not let me attend away matches in London when I was only three years old!

Sheffield United had just hammered Hull City 3 – 0 piling even more pressure on Leeds than even before the Wigan game. It was then that most Whites fans approached this match with the familiar mixture of foreboding mixed with defiance.

Brentford 2 v Leeds United 0

22nd April 2019.

Brentford

Daniels, Ngoyo, Jeanvier, Sorenson, Odubajo, Mokotjo, Sawyers, Henry, Watkins (Da Silva 87), Maupay, Canos (Marcondes 81.)
Unused Substitutes: Racic, Oksanen, Gunnarsson, Forss, Ogbene.

Leeds United

Casilla, Ayling, Jansson (Clarke 64), Cooper, Alioski (Dallas 12), Forshaw, Hernandez, Klich, Roberts (Roofe 58), Harrison, Bamford.
Unused Substitutes: Peacock – Farrell, Beradi, Shackleton, Phillips.

Referee: J Linington

Attendance: 11,580

It was good to see Liam Cooper back in the side but the injury curse struck again as Gianni Alioski hobbled off with a torn cartilage after only twelve minutes. Shortly afterwards, Patrick Bamford was brought down in the penalty area but the referee waved away United's claims. When played back, this was clearly a penalty but it wasn't to be.

United's nemesis, MAUPAY (45) picked up a neat pass from Canos and put Brentford ahead and the Whites fans stated to get that sinking feeling again.

In the second half, Maupay returned the compliment and put CANOS (62) through to end United's hopes of a point.

At the end of the match, many of the Leeds team looked broken. Hernandez couldn't hold back the tears and United could now only achieve automatic promotion if Sheffield United faltered in the last two games. Bielsa took the unprecedented step of comforting each of his players as they left the field.

This time, the pendulum didn't swing, it stuck on Sheffield United's side of the clock, giving them a clear advantage.

Position in Championship after Match: 3rd.

'This is the summary of our season; many chances compared to the goals we actually score. If we had normal efficiency, we would have ten or twelve points more. That is not the case, so we have to put all our energy into the option we still have. As long as mathematics says some-

thing is possible we will be following this but we know that our opportunities were in these last two games.'

Marcelo Bielsa

When United played Aston Villa at home, their fate was all but decided. Sheffield United had beaten Ipswich the previous day and only a set of unlikely circumstances could prevent the Blades from sealing automatic promotion in the second spot.

Leeds United 1 v Aston Villa 1

28th April 2019.

Leeds United

Casilla, Ayling, Jansson, Cooper, Dallas (Beradi 45), Phillips, Hernandez, Forshaw, Klich, Harrison (Roberts 45), Bamford.
Unused Substitutes: Peacock – Farrell, Brown, Shackleton, Bogusz, Clarke.

Aston Villa

Steer, El Mohamady, Tuanzebe, Mings, Taylor, McGinn, Hourihane, Grealish (Whelan 90+1), Green, Kodjia (Jedinak 79), El Ghazi.

Referee: S Attwell

Attendance: 36,786

Any thoughts that this game would play out as a jaded, meaningless encounter were soon dispelled as both sides went about their work with gusto.

As is customary, Leeds had more chances in the first half but Villa had the better ones.

However, it will be the second half that people will remember for years to come. United had started well and were bombarding the the Villa goal with an intensity that continued until the final whistle.

Unfortunately, Premier League referee Stuart Attwell gradually lost control of the game as the Villa players dived, tumbled and writhed in agony before making miraculous recoveries as soon as the whistle was blown. Jack Grealish was the worst offender and it was rumoured that he was appearing on loan from the Royal Shakespeare Company. As the yellow cards were handed out like fliers outside a Dominos Pizza Shop, it seemed inevitable that that something serious was going to happen.

Liam Cooper legitimately tackled Jonathan Kotjia, who stayed down. Maybe Attwell felt that the 'boy had cried wolf' too many times, who knows? Tyler Roberts received the ball from Cooper, paused briefly to check that the game was still in progress and passed the ball to KLICH (72) who weaved his way through what remained of the Villa defence and slotted the ball home to the delight of the home crowd.

All hell then broke loose with Villa players surrounding Klich and throwing punches as the Pole tried to extricate himself from the melee. It was clear that somebody was going to get a red card and Attwell maintained a high level of consistency by handing it to an innocent party. Patrick Bamford had thrown himself to the ground, feigning a non–existent facial injury from a punch which was never thrown. Attwell sent the hapless El Ghazi off, causing more mayhem.

After a stoppage of more than five minutes, Marcelo Bielsa ordered his players to allow Villa to walk an unopposed goal into the net. ADOMAH (77) duly obliged. Only the emotional Pontus Jansson tried to stop him but he was on his own in this.

For the remainder of the game, United continued to press but could not convert their chances.

It was a spirited performance and should have put the Whites in good heart for their final fixture and the forthcoming playoffs.

Much has been said and written about Bielsa's controversial decision to allow Villa to equalise in the bizarre way which they did. It was certainly good sportsmanship but also possibly a very clever ploy to take the moral high ground should theses sides meet again in the play offs.

Position in Championship after Match: 3rd.

'Today's events against the most in form team in the league at the moment puts us close to what our possibilities are.'

Marcelo Bielsa.

Ipswich Town 3 v Leeds United 2

5th May 2019

Ipswich Town

Bialkowski, Bree, Chambers, Nsiala, Kenlock, Downes (Jackson 62), Skuse, Chalobah, Dozzell (Elder 74), Qaner, Judge.
Unused Substitutes: Emmanuel, Gerken, El Mizouni, Brown, Harrison.

Leeds United

Cassilla, Ayling, Jansson, Cooper, Dallas, Phillips, Hernandez, Forshaw, (Clarke61), Klich, Harrison, Roofe.
Unused Substitutes: Peacock – Farrell, Beradi, Edmonson, Shackleton, Bogusz, Gotts.

Referee: G Ward

Attendance: 20,895

Once again, United continued their trend of losing to supposedly inferior teams, succumbing to relegated Ipswich. This led us to ponder why there weren't even more players on the injured list, considering the number of banana skins that they have slipped on this season.

This was a crazy game with crazy incidents. Kiko Cassilla, as he is prone to do, went walkabout outside his area, taking Colin

Qaner down in the process. The keeper was lucky to escape with a yellow card. From the resultant free kick, Alan Judge's delivery bounced out to a grateful DOWNES (30) to put Ipswich ahead.

On the stroke of half time, Forshaw sent Ayling down the right wing with a slightly overhit ball. Somehow he reached it, pulled it back and set KLICH (45) up with a fine equaliser.

Just after the break, Town went ahead again when DOWNES (47) split a sluggish looking defence.

Then it was United's turn as DALLAS (76) helped United draw level after Roofe hit the bar.

Once again, United were battering the home defence, with Jack Clarke being very unlucky not to score with two consecutive attempts.

Four minutes later, Roofe twisted and turned in the Ipswich box before being felled by Luke Chambers, who was sent off for his efforts. The ref pointed to the spot and most Leeds fans were greatly relieved that top scorer Kemar Roofe was back after the previous penalty misses from Bamford and Hernandez.

Although there was no banana skin in the penalty area, Roofe lost his footing and spooned the ball over the bar.

To add insult to injury at the very end of the game, Cassilla and Ayling dithered at the edge of the Leeds penalty area to allow QANER (90) to step in and slot the ball into an empty net. Whether the Spanish keeper was fearful of picking up a second yellow card, we shall never know but it was totally out of character.

In the end it made no difference as United finished the season in third place. Hardly a morale booster though!

'If you put aside the mistakes that we made from this game, the performance from the team was good enough. At the end of the game, you could not think that this opponent could score three goals against us

and it was impossible that we could not score three or four goals.

We conceded three goals and this is something that it is honestly impossible to explain and we also scored only two goals which is also difficult to justify.'

Marcelo Bielsa

CHAPTER 11

The Play Offs

United's finishing position of third brought them Away and Home ties with their old rivals Derby County.

After the experience against Aston Villa, shortly before the first tie, Bielsa announced that he had met with his squad and discussed the policy regarding stopping the game for injuries. They agreed unilaterally that it was solely the Referee's responsibility to stop the game if he felt that a player needed treatment and that in all circumstances, Leeds United would not kick the ball out to stop play.

This simple clarification was, as usual full of common sense and was a clear message to all the divers and play actors that there would be no more free goals from Leeds United.

Derby County 0 v Leeds United 1

11th May 2019.

First Leg Championship Play Off Semi Final Tie.

Derby County

Roos, Bogle, Tomori, Keogh, Malone, Mount, Johnson, Wilson, Holmes (Bennett 70), Lawrence (Huddlestone (89), Nugent (Marriott 64).
Unused Substitutes: Carson,Josefzoon, MacDonald, Evans.

Leeds United

Casilla, Ayling, Beradi, Cooper, Dallas, Phillips, Hernandez, Forshaw (Shackleton (24), Klich, Harrison, Roofe (Clarke 81).
Unused Substitutes: Peacock – Farrell, Strujik, Brown, Bogusz, Gotts.

Referee: C Pawson

Attendance: 31,723

United were back to their irrepressible best and bossed this game from the beginning. Although Pontus Jansson was absent with an ankle injury, Gaetano Beradi reminded us how he had kept the big Swede out of the side earlier in the season by his solid defending and speed in moving the ball out from the back.

Another early injury blow was suffered when Adam Forshaw had to withdraw with what looked like a hamstring problem.

However, the introduction of Jamie Shackleton seemed to energise the Whites.

Dallas came close with a great effort which just cleared the bar but the game stayed tight until the last kick of the first half.

After the break, United continued to dominate the possession. Pablo Hernandez was having a relatively quiet game by his own high standards but Jack Harrison split the Derby defence with a 'Pabloesque' assist, which ROOFE (55) slotted home unerringly. The move had started deep in the Leeds half and was a joy to watch.

Leeds rode a penalty appeal near the end as Jack Harrison tangled with Jayden Bogle. After pointing to the spot, referee Craig Pawson consulted his linesman who persuaded him to overturn his decision.

The Whites looked fresher and sharper than their opponents and will be looking forward to the second leg with a small advantage and high hopes.

Leeds United 2 v Derby County 4

Leeds United

Casilla, Ayling, Cooper, Beradi, Dallas, Phillips, Hernandez, Shackleton, Klich (Clarke 86), Harrison, Bamford (Brown 88). Unused Substitutes: Peacock – Farrell, Bogusz, Gotts, Strujik, Jansson.

Derby County

Roos, Bogle, Keogh, Tomori, Malone, Holmes, (Marriott 44) Johnson, Wilson (Cole 90), Mount, Lawrence, Bennett (Huddlestone 59).

Referee: A Taylor

Attendance: 36,326

Back to Elland Road for the Second Leg: Everybody was singing a song mocking Derby Manager Frank Lampard. A scarf was laid on each seat for people to wave and add to the atmosphere - A packed stadium – Traffic Delays – Deafening noise as the teams came out. The scene was set but as has happened so often in the past, United threw their advantage away.

Leeds started well enough and seemed to be taking control of the tie and the eventual result when DALLAS (24) slotted the ball home to tumultuous applause. Klich later hit the post with a sizzler before disaster struck just before half time. Not for the first time, Casilla went wandering out of his area and in the resultant confusion between himself and Cooper, MARRIOTT (44) nipped in to score.

Shortly after half time, MOUNT (46) brought the sides level over the two ties cracking the ball into the top right corner of the net.

Worse was to come Bennett drew a foul from Cooper in the penalty area and WILSON (58) made no mistake with the subsequent penalty.

Four minutes later DALLAS (62) gave United fresh hope by scoring a lovely goal in front of a grateful Kop.

The game became more and more ill tempered as both sides sought to find the winning solution. Beradi was red carded after picking up a second yellow and United seemed to lose any semblance of defensive shape.

MARRIOTT (85) ran through and chipped the ball over Casilla and into the net for the goal which broke the hearts of the Leeds players and fans. They were beaten after dominating the two ties for more than two hours. How it is possible to squander a two goal lead in the manner they did will be the subject of debate for years to come.

At the end the Leeds team collapsed with exhaustion to the mocking cheers of the Derby fans who could not believe their luck.

'We couldn't finish first or second and we couldn't reach the final. Obviously there are mistakes that prevented us from reaching our goals and when you can't reach something that was reachable, it always puts doubt on the Head Coach.'

Marcelo Bielsa

CHAPTER 12

Bielsa the Man

As the Leeds public took Bielsa to their hearts, many stories were recounted about the man's humility and generosity. Hours spent posing for selfies and autographing shirts for young and old alike were the norm with this incredible guy.

Michael Gill

However, I am indebted to David Burrow of Wetherby, who posted the following piece on You Tube. The story went viral on Twitter because it perfectly encapsulated the essence of Bielsa:

David's Story

'I'm a life long Leeds fan and live in Wetherby, the town closest to Leeds United's Thorpe Arch training complex.

Bielsa also lives in Wetherby and you'll often see him passing through town in the morning. He wears the full Leeds training gear, complete with back pack, making no attempt to go incognito. He is, of course walking the two miles to Thorpe Arch. There is no 'pimped up' limo for him, he sees himself as an ordinary man trying to blend in on his way to work.

In the afternoons, he'll often be spotted sitting in town with his staff in coffee shops. They are all clad in full Leeds training gear and appear to be going over tactics and dealing with paperwork. Unsurprisingly, they often take a break to be photographed with kids.

A few weeks ago, I was driving close to my house and saw a group of slightly dishevelled guys who nearly stepped out into the road right in front of my car. As I prepared to slam on my brakes, I spotted that it was actually Bielsa with a group of his disciples. Thankfully, they stepped back as I drove past. I hesitated for a moment before thinking: "I'll never get a better chance!" So I parked the car and ran over to them.

When he spotted me, Bielsa said "Photo?" and invited me over. One of his colleagues offered to take the snap, even taking the time to ensure that it was framed correctly. He also took it from two different angles to make certain that he got the perfect photo for this (sad?) forty year old man who was thrilled to be getting a memento up close and personal with his latest football idol.

The strangest thing was that five hours later, I received a message from my wife. She was in town with our one week old baby and was meeting a friend for coffee. I opened the message, expecting that it would contain an instruction to pick something up from the Supermarket. Instead it contained a picture of my smiling spouse holding our baby daughter posing with a beaming 'Grandad' Bielsa!

I proudly showed my photos to a fellow Leeds supporting dad the next day after dropping my eldest daughter off at school.

My friend replied: "Oh yeah, he lives in that flat over there."

He was pointing at the most basic, nondescript first floor 'granny' flat that you could imagine.

I believe that it is fair to say that money and glamour do not motivate this man and that we are extremely fortunate to have such a world renowned, yet genuine and humble person as our head coach.

Una Argentina en Leeds – Marta's Story

Marta Parodi rapidly became one of the Leeds Family via Twitter. She lives in her home City of Buenos Aires and is a lifelong supporter of her local team; Velez Sarsfield. She has admired Bielsa as a coach and as a person for more than thirty years. This respect was cemented when Bielsa came to Velez Sarsfield and coached the team when they were Champions in 1998.

Since then she has followed his career wherever he has been in the World.

This is her story:

'When Marcelo Bielsa arrived in Leeds, I already knew something of the club's history but I didn't know anything about the City, the County of Yorkshire or its people.

I researched the internet for more facts but could not really find out what I wanted to know.

Therefore, I connected with the 'Leeds Family' on Twitter and it was 'love at first sight.'

A somewhat 'loca' Argentine that followed Leeds United from Buenos

Michael Gill

Aires wanted to be closer. I wanted to be happy with them and suffer with them as well. I wanted to be a part of everything that was happening.

Four months later, the inevitable happened! I travelled to Leeds to meet my new friends, to sing with them at Elland Road and to visit the places where they see Bielsa passing by every day.

When I arrived in Leeds, I found that it was a beautiful city. I visited its streets, its Churches and its museums.

I was fortunate to have spring sunshine to enjoy the magnificent landscapes of Yorkshire. I visited the historic city of York and the Bronte House at Haworth. "Jane Eyre" is one of my favourite books and I was thrilled to read excerpts from it on the walls of the Museum.

How green and luminous is Yorkshire, how charming is Leeds and how loving and kind its people.

This was my first time in Leeds and I'm sure that there will be more times. I arrived in Leeds following Bielsa but Leeds got inside me.

There are loves that never end!

CHAPTER 13

Conclusions

And so it is over. The marathon race that is the EFL Championship has now come to an end.
Even back in the 1950's, the Second Tier was known as 'The Cockpit of Football.'

I started watching Leeds in 1958 and have seen them relegated from the top flight three times.

I have only seen them promoted to the top tier twice.

It took the great Don Revie three seasons before his emerging side went up as Champions in the 1963 – 64 season.

Howard Wilkinson led his side to the 'promised land' in his second season when they were Champions in 1989 – 1990.

These managers both had very different personalities although neither could be described as flamboyant.

Bielsa is different again but he has also failed in his first attempt to put the Whites back where they belong. Nevertheless, he has built firm foundations that should help with United's success in the very near future.

Of course nowadays, this is an even bigger challenge as the constant search for instant success continues and Head Coaches move from club to club after very short periods in charge. This managerial carousel occurs at all levels of the game. Despite the fact that changing managers after very short periods is proven to be totally ineffective, Clubs search for a panacea that is going to put everything right. They rarely find it.

Marcelo Bielsa's achievements at Leeds are overshadowed by the fact that the team led the league for so many weeks and months before failing at the final hurdle.

Nevertheless, to properly evaluate Bielsa's achievements, we should look at the unprecedented number of injuries to the first team squad. One of the reasons that more has not been made of this is because Marcelo has never moaned about it or tried to use it as an excuse. It is hard to imagine that many of his contemporaries behaving in the same manner.

Listed below are players from the First Team Squad along with the number of games that they have been unavailable for selection because of injury:

Bailey Peacock – Farrell	1
Jack Harrison	1
Pontus Jansson	4
Jack Clarke	8
Luke Ayling	7
Pablo Hernandez	7
Liam Cooper	10
Kemar Roofe	14
Adam Forshaw	16
Barry Douglas	22
Stuart Dallas	21
Patrick Bamford	22
Gaetano Beradi	24
Gianni Alioski	4

One thing that Revie, Wilkinson and Bielsa have in common is their commitment to the development of young players.

The Under 23 Development Squad run by Carlos Corberan won the Premier Development League title despite the fact that a high number of their players were 'borrowed' to play in the First Team because of the injury situation.

Corberan himself split his duties between the First Team and Development Squad, ensuring a seamless link between the two. Needless to say, Bielsa showed a keen interest, often appearing at matches and sometimes mixing in with the other spectators.

The Under 18 squad, managed by Mark Jackson unsurprisingly ended as Runners Up in their league also.

Therefore a structure is in place and the scene is set for the future. All of the squads play exactly the same method of attacking football and it is therefore a simple task for players to step up when this is required of them.

Bielsa has united the city of Leeds again. We did not choose him. He chose us and we are proud that he did.

There is so much more that I could say but this book cannot end without saying: 'Thank you Marcelo from the bottom of our hearts.'

Michael Gill 16th May 2019.

AUTHOR'S NOTE:

One of the most rewarding parts of this 'labour of love,' was to read again the words of wisdom that flow off the tongue of this man. A Championship season consists of no fewer than forty six games and I have harvested a quotation from Bielsa for every one of them.

I cannot imagine how boring this would have been had I quoted virtually any other football manager. The repetitive, clichéd nonsense that most of them spout week after week is so predictable that I could have made them all up myself. Not so with Marcelo!

Every quotation is verbatim and if the grammar suffers because of the translation, I still feel that it is a more honest way of recording his words.

ILLUSTRATIONS

Tickets for the Celestial Premier League

The Piper

Quentin - Landlord of the White Hart

Matt, Wendy and Andy

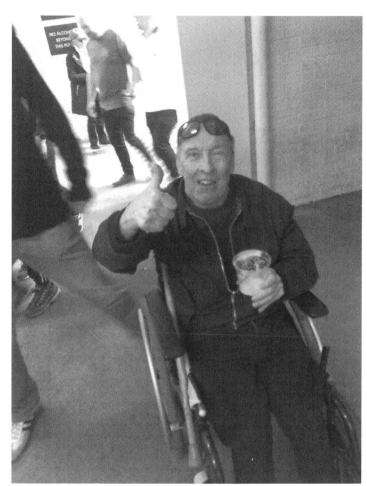

Macker

Ethan & Steve

Stoke City v Leeds August 1962

Michael Gill

Ad for Joules 1962 - Stoke City Programme

Birmingham Irish Centre

Bielsa with David Burrow

'Grandad' Bielsa with Jacki Burrow & Baby

Printed in Great
Britain
by Amazon